World Cup Ski Technique

Learn and Improve

James Major and Olle Larsson

Poudre Publishing Company

Box 181 • LaPorte, Colorado • 80535

Original Title: World Cup Ski Technique, Learn and Improve
Copyright © Editions Buchheim, Fribourg, Switzerland

First Edition

T11/79

Photographs by Olle Larsson and James Major.
1978 Madonna di Campiglio and Kitzbuhel with the photographic
assistance of Lars Larsson.

Photomontages: Olle Larsson
Photo reproduction: Vaccari, Modena, Italy
Design: Editions Buchheim, Fribourg, Switzerland

Library of Congress Cataloging in Publication Data

Larsson, Olle and James Major
   World Cup Ski Technique

   1. Skis and Skiing.   2. Ski Racing.
Library of Congress Catalog Card No.: 79-90395
ISBN 0-935240-00-4

Printed in the United States of America

Poudre Publishing Company
Box 181
LaPorte, Colorado   80535

Without the scientific and practical knowledge that we gained during our years of study at the University of Grenoble this book could never have been done. Therefore we dedicate this work to our Professor.

Georges Joubert

Acknowledgements

We remain deeply appreciative of the help that we have received all along the way from the following:

The Canadian Alpine Ski Team, Family Larsson, Family Major, Dr. Axel Kentsch, Brit-Marie Persson, Director Kevin Kearny, Andrea Haaser, Uli and Helmut Schmalzl; photographers Sven Gilsaeter, Armando Trovati, Zin Shiga, Lars and Goete Karlsson and Erik Nilsson; Laboratories Colorphoto AB, Goeteborg; Studio 13, Zurich; Kempert and Engert, Munich.

Nippon Kogaku KK and the Service Course, Skis Rossignol S.A.; the organizers of the following World Cup races: Val d'Isere, Garmisch-Partenkirchen, Chamonix, Aspen, Arosa, Aare, Crans-Montana, Oslo, Madonna di Campiglio, Voss, Heavenly Valley, Megeve, Solynieve, Waterville Valley, Bormio, Laax and Sun Valley.

World Cup Ski Technique

Contents

The Authors

Olle Larsson and James Major are both active ski coaches who work with every level of skiers. Recently they have been coaches on the World Cup for the national ski teams of Canada and Norway. Themselves past racers, they have also received scientific education in sports and alpine skiing at the University of Grenoble, France.

Well known for their continuous search for better understanding of the sport, their knowledge and advice is published in the international ski press and read by millions of skiers in Europe and North America.

Olle Larsson and James Major have perfected a very specialized photographic technique which enables skiing movements to be both better understood and learned. Armed with camera, motor and lens, they are a well-known presence at international ski races all over the world.

INTRODUCTION

Can you become a better skier by reading a book? The extent of your interest directly determines how much you will learn from a book and improve. A book can be interesting, but can you, in fact, improve your skiing from a book? As we began to organize the material, 22,000 negatives and as many ideas, we became convinced that the information we will present in this exceptional format can benefit all skiers, whatever their level of skill or degree of commitment to alpine skiing.

It is well known that the best way for the world's elite to improve in a technical sport is to have them train together. The sight of such World Cup winners as Gustavo Thoeni and Piero Gros skiing on the same hill has struck many observers. They improve by copying certain technical elements from one another. This is also true in other sports besides skiing. Tennis's champions Bjorn Borg and Guillermo Vilas trained together and mutually improved. This characteristic of learning by elite athletes is also applicable to the amateur and even the beginner. What is taking place on the snow or the tennis court is nothing more complicated than simple imitation.

Imitation leading to improvement or to failure (imitating faults) in a sport can be done without an understanding of what you are doing differently. The intellect does not need to be involved. This fast and sure method of progress for elite athletes is also possible for all skiers with a certain level of physical condition.

In other words, do we offer something for everyone? We should make it clear this book is *not* for total beginners. New comers to the sport of skiing will not find here advice on how to choose equipment, ride a ski lift, or buckle their ski boots. But those who are already skiers will find insights to progress, whatever their "intermediate" or "advanced" level. With modern ski schools, snow grooming techniques, equipment and teaching methods the beginner's period is very short.

Therefore, we feel strongly that something should be done for those who ski, but wish to ski better; to benefit from the new techniques which have been invented and perfected by the world's best skiers.

Unfortunately we cannot all ski beside Thoeni, Gros, Stenmark, Klammer or Moser-Proell, nor play tennis with Borg. Therefore we felt the only way that this extraordinary visual-transfer process could be offered to everyone is through a book, using as many pictures as possible of the best skiing by the best skiers in the world. Perhaps you may protest that these racers are skiing gates, unlike most skiers. But world class skiers make no extra movements for the slalom pole. At most they will bring the inside arm closer to the body so that it will not catch the gate, but more often the arm is already quite naturally placed for slipping past the pole. Besides, anyone who has ever had the opportunity to observe World Cup skiers in deep or broken snow knows that they are truly the world's best free skiers. The cream of the World Cup all use the same elements of ski technique, regardless of what national team they belong to. They must constantly experiment and improve their technique by trial-and-error and through the help of their coaches. Their search is simply to find the most efficient way of turning their skis. World Cup skiing technique in use today, the public will want several years hence. Racing is the technical vanguard of skiing, and should be the model for all ski instruction.

Since progress by imitation takes place without intellectualization, the reader will benefit from the pictures directly. The photomontage, providing a greater opportunity to dissect movement than, say, a videotape recording or movie, gives the simplest and most immediate learning of all. What, then, is the purpose of the text? Exploiting this advantage of the photomontage, we will direct your attention to the salient details where imitation will most likely pay off.

It would be unreasonable to hope that the untrained eye will always catch the important technical element. With the help of the text, you should be able to focus of the key aspects of a particular champion's technique while passing over the peculiarities of his or her personal style. Eventually, these details will become apparent on the hill and on the television screen as the reader's eye becomes trained. Further, the text can give a pedagogical analysis of the best ski technique. The why, where, when and how are discussed in the light of physiology, anatomy, physics and mechanics and in accordance with the rules and laws which explain human movement.

This may sound complicated, but actually is based on common sense and experience. This, after all, is not a scientific work, but an attempt to show clearly what the best are doing and what you can do to ski more like them. Through the combination of photomontage and text, many misunderstandings, legends and misconceptions about the movements of skiing can be dispelled.

In part I we discuss problems that keep the skier from having the freedom and control of a world class racer. In part II we show what the best skiers do to overcome these problems, because the basic difficulties of alpine skiing are common to all skiers.

There are many different opinions on how to ski. It is our feeling that the photos give proof to the text which can clarify this discussion.

CHAPTER I
The Alpine World Cup

The FIS World Cup of alpine skiing, created in 1967, is without a doubt responsible for the fantastic explosion of interest in ski racing and alpine skiing in general. From its infancy the World Cup has developed into what the Europeans call the "white circus", covering four continents and running from the first week in December until the last weekend in March. World Cup races have been held in the Alps and Spain, Scandinavia and Eastern Europe as well as North America and Japan.

The World Cup organizes alpine ski racing into a coherent circuit which, correspondingly, has boosted interest and popularity. It has absorbed the glamorous "classics" of January; the Arlberg-Kandahar, the Lauberhorn at Wengen and Kitzbuhel's Hahnenkammrennen, and now prolongs interest in ski racing until late spring. It expands every season, and sustains momentum during the year in between the Olympic Games and the FIS World Championships. The elite skiers hold that the winner of the World Cup, determined by amassing points in World Cup sanctioned races throughout the season, is clearly the year's best skier.

By bringing the best skiers in the world to countries where alpine skiing does not have a strong tradition, the World Cup has helped to popularize the sport. It is perhaps one of the best examples in modern times of international elite and mass sport working hand in hand, building both greater participation and an ever stronger elite. The increase in active and spectator interest in ski racing has been paralleled by an increase in the efforts of the skiers, their coaches and the national

ski teams to ski well. The World Cup has been responsible for the dramatic evolution of alpine skiing, its training, ski technique, the equipment, and even of ski areas. The 1978 budget increase of the U.S. and Austrian ski teams is a good example of recent developments: a jump to approximately 1.4 million dollars each, while even more money was spent by the world's largest ski manufacturers' international racing services on their racers for that year.

This is not to mention the countless hours of volunteer labor that go into organizing the races at every level, from "Donald Duck" to the World Cup, or into training of the club champions who later might become World Cup winners.

There is still a long way to go before the World Cup attains the same level as the Formula One automobile world championship to which it is often contrasted, but such figures represent an extraordinary development for alpine skiing, measured against the situation before the World Cup was created. The larger teams include skiers, coaches, leaders, ski and binding technicians as well as the doctors and physiotherapists totalling as many as 30, while the smallest teams from one of the "developing" alpine nations may number as few as two. All together, they comprise starting fields of between 80 and 100 skiers per race.

The skiers start in World Cup races according to an international seeding list published by the FIS which ranks the skiers according to their past results in international competitions. Outside of the elite groups the level of performance rapidly descends, but is improving every season as the competition becomes tougher and tougher.

The present World Cup program matches the same exceptional athletes every week-end throughout the winter. It is impossible for the best to hide what they are doing, and for the losers to cover their mistakes or create excuses. A 1/100 of a second mistake at every gate will often result in a one second difference at the end of a World Cup race - frequently the difference between first and tenth place.

The '78 season created a real elite in the downhill event. Traditionally one of the most selective World Cup downhills, Kitzbuhel's Hahnenkammrennen, in 1978, ended with 4/100 of a second seperating 1st and 4th place, and only one second between 1st and 11th place. This in a race that is more than two minutes long!

To maintain this high level of athletic achievement, year round strenuous training is necessary. Before the first race of Ingemar Stenmark's incredible 1978 season

(when he won the World Cup by the end of January with back-to-back victories in the first six races, going on to become double world champion) he spent over 80 days on skis; training, free-skiing and testing equipment during the preceeding summer and fall.

The girls train and race almost as hard as the boys. They are usually younger, but the very best ski at a level not far from the top 50 men. Husbands do not seem to be a disadvantage, as some of the most succesful women of today's World Cup are happily married. The differences in performance between the men and women in alpine skiing can be explained primarily by the smaller number of women competing internationally.

The winter-long confrontation of the elite of alpine skiing has rendered obvious to all a fact long known to ski technicians: That good skiing is truly international. The first group in the World Cup in slalom includes skiers from the United States, Bulgaria, Yugoslavia and Lichtenstein as well as Austria, Switzerland, Italy and Germany; all using the same elements of technique to ski! The dynamics of skiing to be exploited (in order to get down the hill), their anatomy, and the equipment they use is the same for all of these talented athletes. On the World Cup there are no "national techniques" as exist in the national ski schools. Faced with the same external conditions and the same course, World Cup skiers naturally attempt to use the same efficient skiing technique. The skiers also watch each other very closely, copying and experimenting with what seems to be efficient in other skiers' movements.

The aparent differences in the best skiers' gestures, their personal "styles", are more often than not the sum total of what technical elements are dominating or are missing from their skiing. This directly influences their performance in World Cup competitions, and is the source of remarks often heard, that so-and-so is only good on steep or flat courses, soft snow, or ice, etc. A skier like Ingemar Stenmark who is technically complete can win one giant slalom on pure ice and a short time later win another in flatter, soft snow conditions.

Alpine skiing is an inherently technical sport and the importance of ski technique to all skiers can best be shown by the extreme attention given by World Cup skiers to their technique: the summer-long technical training on skis, the extensive viewing of movies of their competitors, video-tapes of their own skiing and the corrections of their trainers. In spite of this, serious technical faults still exist. Surprisingly, even in the first group of the World Cup, problems are shown with such basic technical elements as hip angulation or rotation. The men are much stronger and more aggressive, but technically not much more advanced than the women. But as awareness of the problems of ski technique grows, and new teaching aids such as video-tape and photomontage become more widely used, the technical level will surely improve.

The statistics show that Ingemar Stenmark is one of the most succesful World Cup skiers ever, having won the last three overall World Cup titles and in 1978 becoming double world champion as well. In World Cup ski races the skiers are trying so hard and taking such enormous risks that it is not uncommon for fewer than 40% of the starting field to make it to the finish. But in spite of the impressive number of Stenmark's victories, he also has a record of finishes in the first ten places unequaled by any other skier. In the past two seasons he has fallen in only two World Cup slaloms. Besides being one of the most consistently succesful, our study material also shows Ingemar Stenmark to be World Cup skiing's most technically perfect skier.

Coincidence? Not at all. Stenmark's consistent success would only be possible with this solid technique, which allows him to attack the course in race after race with a sufficient margin for safety. Ingemar's technique makes it possible for him to finish with the best even on the days when he is not in form. For this reason, much of the demonstration in this book is by Ingemar Stenmark. This model sportsman personifies athletic, technical and moral qualities that all can learn from.

**CHAPTER II
Skiing Mechanics**

The Mechanics of Skiing

An analysis of the technique of any sport must begin with an observation of the best athletes. The greatest problem in analyzing alpine ski technique is that, like all technical disciplines, skiing involves coordinated actions on *several planes at once,* resulting in complex motions, difficult to describe. The tight interaction of the body parts makes an overall view of the skier's movements the most comprehensible. Only then do the problems of timing and coordination become as visible as those of the individual gestures.

Our system of 24x36mm. format motorized photography and photomontage, using a specially built Nikon camera, is a powerful analytical tool. But an effective understanding of the annual evolution of the elite level of skiing also requires a full grasp of the "biomechanical" foundations of the movements. "Biomechanics" is the application of the laws of force and motion to the movements of the human body, in this case the actions of skiing. For example, in 1974 Piero Gros influenced World Cup skiing with a technique that made frequent use of a very important up-motion (extension) between turns. This made such a strong impression that many other elite skiers copied Gros, largely because he was winning. However, with a combined knowledge of ski technique and biomechanics, one could have judged whether this technique was effective or not, and if his extension was, in fact, why Piero was the best at that time.

Skiing is sliding and, although like all other movements is governed by the laws of force and motion (mechanics), it is *not* instinctive to man. (A non-skier's reaction to the feet slipping is very different from that of a skier!) The basic problem of skiing is to remain in balance on the skis while leaving them a maximum of freedom to slide smoothly where you want to go. Therefore, there can be no static positions in good skiing, only movements. A skier's technique is his repertoire of actions which determine how he will respond to the constantly changing situations to be overcome while sliding down a slope. The skier with the

better technique obviously has a greater repertoire of responses. These responses are the "elements" of alpine ski technique.

Ski technique is extremely difficult to analyze correctly, because of the many different planes of movement and the constantly changing external conditions beyond the control of the skier, such as terrain, snow conditions, bumps and holes.

In this chapter we will point out some interesting concepts that will help give an understanding of the photosequences and the skiing. To use the study materials in this book, the reader must keep in mind the following basic characteristics of today's best skiers:

1. the lower body and feet are ready to move rapidly in any direction.
2. the upper body, with its greater mass, is characterized by minimal movement, the arms quietly maintaining balance.
3. both the upper and lower body function together around a kind of universal joint made of the lower back (lumbar) and hip (coxo-femoral) joints together.

►

The two photos to the right represent distinctly different phases of a turn which, due to the forces involved, pose unique problems for the skier. In the upper photo, centrifugal force (horizontal arrow) generated by the turn tends to pull the skier to the outside. The resultant of centrifugal force and gravity (vertical arrow) represents the weighting of the skis (placed on edge to "bite" the snow and resist the outward pull of centrifugal force) and is indicated by the dashed line.

In the lower photo, taken toward the end of a turn, centrifugal force acts in the same direction as the horizontal component of gravity. As a result, centrifugal and gravitational forces combine to pull the skier to the outside of the turn and tend to make the skis side-slip. It is at this moment where one meets the difference between skiers; those who control their skis and the forces involved and the less skilled who submit because of deficient techniques.

The manner in which the forces of skiing act on a skier make certain moments of a turn more difficult than others. These forces determine the movements that must be made and their timing, rendering some techniques more effective than others. The skier can not escape the effect of these forces, but can balance them to maintain a stable equilibrium. It follows that the best skiers in the world tend to use the same technical gestures to overcome the difficulties of the race course.

The photomontages on the following two pages were taken during the first run of the 1977 Hahnenkamm slalom in Kitzbuhel, Austria and show the readily observable similarities in movements of two of the world's best skiers, Piero Gros of Italy and Ingemar Stenmark from Sweden. In this particular run they posted *exactly* the same time to a hundredth of a second.

Ingemar Stenmark, Sweden: Kitzbuhel slalom, 1977.
Conditions: drop-off to a moderate slope. Falling fresh snow.

1. Balance on skis

The phenomenon of human balance enables us to walk upright and keeps us from falling down with every motion. To better understand the special balance of the skier, we must first discuss the physiology involved.

Balancing is a reflex action of the body relying on impulses received from balance information centers; the inner ear, sight of the horizon (visual cues), pressure under the soles of the feet, the position of the joints and the state of tension of certain muscles or muscle groups in acting to keep the skeleton upright. These impulses trigger contraction reflexes which pull the body into a balanced position. This in turn creates new impulses which slow down this pull by contraction of the opposite group of muscles, called antagonists, so that the body is not pulled too far. The result of this reflex action is an oscillation slightly in and out of balance, constant except when lying down. There is no "balanced position" as such, because good balance is a very dynamic process. This is true for the skier as well, but in a much more energetic way as the forces tending to throw him or her out of balance are much greater.

There is an important difference between the experienced and beginning skier's balancing mechanisms. The beginner keeps himself upright by supporting himself against the boots, the tips and tails of the skis, the right and left ski and even the ski poles. If the beginner starts to fall backward, he can push against the back of the boots and the tails of the skis, and when losing balance forward, he uses the support of the tongue of the boot. Should he fall to the left, he steps on the left ski, etc.. A good skier does this also (albeit more subtly), but, more importantly, he catches his balance by pushing against *himself*, using other parts of the body for support in much the same way that a cat, dropped on its back, will be able to turn in the air, always landing on its feet.

Expert skiers have a sixth sense - "intelligence of the feet", Olympic and World Cup champion Jean-Claude Killy called it. All of their movements are conditioned

Piero Gros, Italy:
Kitzbuhel slalom, 1977.

by what is happening at the level of the contact between their skis and the snow. Instead of skiing by "position" they ski with their feet. Information is picked up by the soles of the feet in the boots and movements are initiated by the feet and legs, instead of the upper body. This snow sense is also the secret to good sliding.

Perhaps the beginner has an image to follow from what he has seen (or believes to have seen) better skiers do, or perhaps from what his instructor has taught him. This image must now be translated into movement. As the gesture has probably not been well defined by the brain, the mind sends too many commands to the muscles, resulting in stiff and uncoordinated movements, accompanied by the fight to keep from falling as well. Trying to keep upright often triggers even more muscular impulses from the balance system. Because of having to work many more muscles than the good skier, it is understandable that the beginner becomes more tired in a shorter time.

Physiological research also shows that a good skier and a beginner use their muscles in different ways. The muscular contractions of a good skier are briefer but more violent, allowing for more relaxation than the beginner, whose muscles contract more weakly but for longer periods of time. However, as the beginning skier becomes more proficient through practice, the

movements become better defined in the nervous system until the stage of automatic reaction is reached. Each command to the muscle will no longer have to be consciously thought out. As practice continues, only the muscles which are absolutely necessary are given commands by the nervous system to contract, thereby avoiding the stiffness and staticness common to so many beginners.

Because balance is a reflex effort, the reaction time of the muscles becomes very important. Physiological research reveals that both very relaxed and very tensed muscles are relatively slow to react. The fastest results are obtained by muscles under the constant, but slight, tension related to maintaining normal posture. It should be clear that extremely upright or low positions hamper good balance on skis.

Skiing balance is a problem caused by the sensation of sliding received by the feet, eyes and inner ear. The body's natural reaction is to stiffen the legs and try to dig in the heels, that is, to stop the slipping. This is absolutely the wrong reaction for good skiing. By concentration and training, the skier must learn to relax, bend the legs slightly and let the skis slide freely while distributing the body's weight over the entire foot. Since the well-fitting ski boot locks the foot flat to the sole, the beginning skier must become accustomed to moving without flexing the foot and toes as in normal walking and running. As the sensation of sliding becomes more natural through training, the joy of freedom that is alpine skiing can be experienced.

Center of Mass

The skier's center of mass (CM) is the focal point for the forces of balance. It can be found internally or externally and because of the weight of the skis, boots, and bindings, it is lower than in a non-skier. By moving parts of the body, such as the feet, arms, or hips, the skier can move the CM around; higher, lower, forward, backward and to the sides. This is important for maintaining balance, anticipating problem situations or preparing special gestures.

There is another important aspect, however, of the mobility of the center of mass. Every movement of the body moves the CM, which then requires the body to react to regain balance with the CM in its new position. Therefore, every unnecessary movement is ultimately bad for the stability and balance of the skier. The center of mass of the poor skier moves suddenly and jerkily because of extra, unnecessary movements that, then, create great balance problems. One of the reasons for the exceptional stability of a good skier or racer is that his center of mass moves much more smoothly in and around his body and down the slope. The way the best

World Cup skiers calmly and quietly ski is noticed by all spectators. Therein lies one of their secrets of smooth, safe and efficient skiing.

The base of support

The skier must react constantly to the forces which would make him fall. To stay in balance the resultant of all of the forces acting on the skier (or more specifically on the center of mass of the skier) must fall within the area of support (the polygon of sustentatin).

The polygon of sustentation is all of the area between the points of support of the body. For a skier this polygon is quite large because of the length of the skis. The wider the stance between the legs, the better the support and balance. Planting the pole to the side also increases the area enormously.

The balance of a skier is better when the force necessary to push him out of balance (such that the

sustentation. Practically, this means that by moving the upper body or the feet or *both* the skier can quickly catch his balance or, for the expert, avoid coming out of balance.

As the balance pole is to the circus tight-rope walker, so are the arms and ski poles to the skier. By their position out to the side of the body they provide both stability *and* the possibility to remain in balance if a fall starts. To rapidly react they should not be too contracted nor too relaxed, neither completely hanging down nor stuck out to the side like wings.

CM is no longer over his polygon of sustentation) must be ever greater. The bigger the polygon of sustentation, the more the CM can be moved and still remain over the area of support. For the skier going straight or turning, this polygon can rapidly be made larger by spreading the feet or planting the ski pole. Lowering the CM over the area of support has the same effect, making the skier more stable.

The skier must often move the point the forces of skiing are acting upon to keep it over the area of support, by moving either the CM or the polygon of

2. The forces of skiing

Straight down and turning

A skier sliding straight down is held to the slope by a component of the force of gravity acting perpendicular to the slope (FGPr). He is pulled down the slope by a component of the force of gravity parallel to the slope (FGPl). The actions of these two forces on the skier's center of mass produce his speed.

These forces are opposed by drag produced by the friction between the skis and the snow (FrS) and the friction of the air (FrA). When FrS and FrA together equal FGPl, then there is constant speed. However, if FGPl is greater than FrS + FrA, then the skier experiences acceleration, and when FrA + FrS is greater than FGPl, the skier slows down.

These same forces act on the skier while turning as during straight running, however, two new forces are introduced. Turning creates *centrifugal force* (CF) which pulls the skier along a tangent to the outside of the turn. To continue turning, the skier must resist, or create a *centripetal force* (CpF). The skier does this with

a combination of technical elements such as leaning to the inside of the turn and angulating to dig the edges into the snow, and muscle power.

In many ways, the forces acting upon a bicyclist and a skier are very similar. To resist centrifugal force both a skier and a bicycle rider must lean their bodies toward the inside of the turn. However, the skier bends and twists to angulate rather than bank into the turn as completely as does the bicyclist. It is relatively easy to balance on a bicycle because the tires do not slip sideways as readily.

The difficulty of skiing gates as compared to free skiing is that the skier cannot change the line of his turn in order to compensate for the forces generated. He can't go wherever his momentum carries him, but must change his angulation according to the gates. In practice, this means changing the angle of the skis in relation to the snow surface, making the skis bite the snow to hold a particular line through the gates. However, this is also true for the good recreational skier who wants to ski down difficult terrain and for safety's sake must have

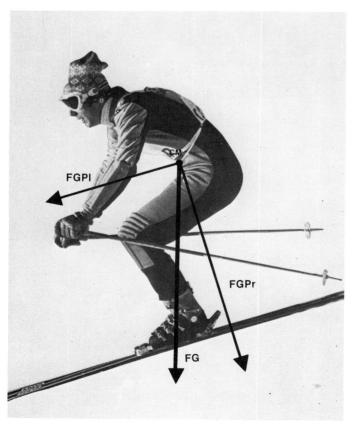

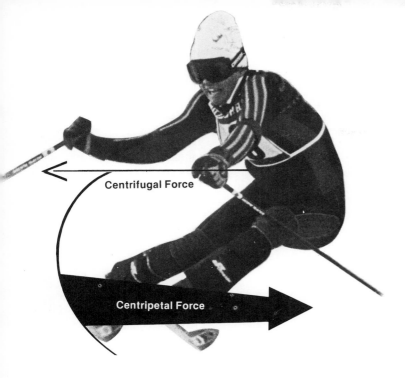

Centrifugal Force

Centripetal Force

good control. The feet, knees and hip enable the skier to constantly adjust his angulation for controlled skiing.

The balance of a skier is best when the resultant of the forces of gravity and the forces which are pulling the body to the outside and down the hill pass through the outside ski. The bicyclist is also in balance when the resultant of forces pulling out and pulling down passes exactly through the tires. The skier has an advantage which the bicyclist does not: the polygon of sustentation of a bicyclist is limited to the tires, and if they slip, then the rider goes down with no chance of saving himself. But the skier, with the feet apart, pushing solidly on the outside ski, can quickly stand on the inside ski which is left underneath his body should the outside ski stop holding. It is interesting to note that if the skier tries to ski with his feet close together (small base of support), or on the inside ski, this safety factor is forfeited.

Inertia

The most important characteristic of modern ski technique is that the feet are ready to move rapidly while the upper body is stable and calm. The reason for this lies in the *relative inertia* of these two segments of the body. Most of the body weight is concentrated above the waist.

The arms and their position play a particular role. Due to the longer lever produced when the arms are held out to the side of the body, their inertia becomes much greater and, subsequently, their stabilizing influence on the upper body is increased.

A good illustration of this principle is that of the figure skater performing a spin. If the skater starts the spin with the arms held close to the body but then extends them out to the side, an immediate deceleration occurs. If the arms are returned to their original position, then the speed immediately increases again. The arms in a horizontal position increase the inertia of the upper body. Having more weight, and therefore greater inertia, the upper body requires greater force to get into motion.

Correspondingly, once it is moving to a new position, it also requires more force and more time to stop. The lower body, even with the skis, boots and bindings, is relatively light. Less energy and less time is required for movements of the feet, knees and legs. Greater finesse with less effort is possible.

The good skier avoids these problems when it is necessary to move the upper body by anticipating what will have to be done. In this way, the good skier will start to position his body before this position is actually needed to balance the forces involved. Smooth skiing with a minimum of effort from the skier is the result of these techniques.

Anticipation is very natural, just as in walking when the upper body tilts forward before the step is taken. The trunk of the walker's body is already in position before the legs are moved. The skier also has the choice of changing the relative position of his CM by moving his feet; forward, backward or from side to side, instead of his upper body. The effect is the same.

Horizontal Plane

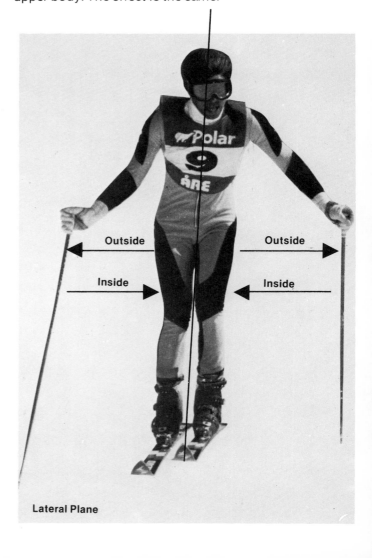

Outside   Outside

Inside   Inside

Lateral Plane

3. Technical foundations.

In the most fundamental sense, ski technique can be reduced to movements that turn or pivot the skis, bank them onto edge, and adjust the distribution of pressure placed on them while keeping the body mass in balance. The movements can be complex and varied and the techniques of the current champions are distinguished by their wide range of movement patterns in all directions.

At times, it's convenient to describe these intricate movement patterns in relation to the axes and planes around or along which they move. There are three planes, a horizontal plane and two vertical planes. The horizontal plane bisects the skier into upper and lower halves of equal mass. Since the upper and lower segments are equal, the horizontal plane must pass through the skier's center of mass.

Likewise, both of the vertical planes pass through the center of mass but are oriented at right angles to each other. The lateral plane bisects the skier into right and left sides and the fore-aft plane bisects the skier into front and back halves of equal mass.

The movements of skiing can be described in relation to these planes but rotary or pivoting movements are better discussed in relation to axes of rotation; a vertical axis, a lateral-horizontal axis and a fore-aft horizontal axis. Angulation, for example, involves movements in two planes and around two axes at the same time; a twisting of the body around the hip and a flexion of the waist. The twist of the hip is a rotation in the horizontal plane around the vertical axis and the waist flexion is a movement in the fore-aft plane with the upper body rotating around the lateral axis.

The movements are powered by the muscles or gravity, or both, acting to move the joints. When two different body segments surrounding a joint move closer to each other, the movement is called a *flexion*; when they straighten out, an *extension*. These two terms are often used in discussing ski technique. To be more precise, they refer only to action at a single joint, but they're often used to describe larger movements involving much of the body, such as flexion or extension unweighting.

The muscles that straighten a joint are called extensors and those that flex or bend a joint are called flexors. If both groups operate on the same joint, they are antagonists.

The antagonists play an important role in the coordination and control of movements. In the vigorous movements of skiing, the antagonists often become so involved in slowing down a motion and preventing an exaggeration of the movement that when the movement is completed the return to a basic stance or new movement becomes even more energetic as the antagonist takes over as the principle force acting on the joint. The coordinated movements of the flexors and extensors on the different joints compose the

Fore-Aft Plane

Hip angulation

Hip angulation

technical motions of skiing. On the purely muscular level, when these muscle groups are linked, rhythmic and efficient skiing is possible.

Gravity alone can extend a joint or cause its flexion if the muscles are suddenly relaxed. In a body flexion, gravity can be assisted by the muscle power of the flexors to accelerate the down motion.

A body extension, such as the extension of upunweighting, involves all of the most important extensor muscle groups of the body with a corresponding *press* on the skis as the body rises against gravity. When the ankles, knees, hips and back flex and extend, a forward and backward movement over the skis is produced.

All of these joints, except the knee, can also twist or rotate to displace segments of the body sideways. The knee moving laterally, as in knee angulation, is the result of a double rotation; first at the hip socket and then in the ankle. The knee can only bend and straighten because of the strong, tight ligaments which block any lateral flexing at the knee joint. All of these joints are well supplied with nerves which monitor their movements and the degree of bending under the direction of the balance and information centers of the nervous system.

The back is relatively stiff, bending backward or to either side, but has excellent capabilities for twisting (around the vertical axis) and bending forward. This means that during anticipation and angulation, the upper body twists instead of bending sideways. For this reason, the body remains very supple, even when strongly angulated. This would not be the case, of course, if it were only necessary for the upper body to tilt sideways in order to place the weight over the outside ski.

The hips are ball and socket joints which allow a great deal of movement in all directions. The hips are equipped with strong muscles for standing up, bending down and twisting.

The ankle joints allow the foot to bend and the leg to twist. Modern ski boots stiffen the ankle and provide support but should never completely restrict flexibility or rotation.

Angulation and anticipation are twisting-bending movements of the skier which displace the center of mass from side to side along the lateral plane. The term angulation refers to the angle formed by the axes of the upper and lower body when the waist is flexed and rotated over the outside hip joint. This is commonly referred to as hip angulation and is clearly demonstrated in World Cup racing to be the most effective way of making the edges hold, the skis carve and the skier remain supple while still resisting the forces of the turn.

Knee angulation is a very different manuever where

Knee angulation

the knee is flexed and the entire leg rotated inward at the hip and ankle. The angle formed by the axes of the calf and thigh is very evident. This movement makes it possible to edge the ski quickly, but the thigh and calf are no longer aligned and the knee can no longer flex to absorb bumps and holes. Since the muscles of the knee are much weaker than the muscles around the hip joint, knee angulation must last a comparatively short time. Knee angulation also places great stress on the knee joint; held in this position principally by the inside lateral ligaments which must alone absorb considerable weight and pressure.

In a carved turn, the tip and tail of the carving ski follow almost exactly the same path. A sideslipped turn places the skis more or less across the direction of travel, the tails following a path outside of the path followed by the tips. Either way, the shape of the skis produces a tendency to keep turning.

The friction between the skis and the snow can be very much higher, however, for a sideslipping ski than a carving ski. A ski that is carving allows for both better sliding and greater control than a skidding ski. There is no one secret for making a ski carve, but every element of good technique discussed in this book comes into play. World Cup skiers, incidentally, are the best in the world at making their skis carve through turns.

It would be a mistake to assume that there exists a "model turn" or "perfect line" for all conditions. Good technique allows a skier to find the most efficient way to ski over flat or steep terrain, ice or powder snow, making fast or slow turns.

The steepest line down a slope is the fall line. A complete turn, which crosses the fall line two times, can be divided into distinct phases with different problems to be overcome by the skier in each phase. In the first phase (I) of the turn, the skier must accomplish a change from one set of edges to the other and project his center of mass toward the next turn. This can involve technically complicated manuevers, but good coordination and timing can lessen the amount of effort needed by the skier.

In the next two phases (II and III), the skier must carve the skis through the turn. Most of the gross technical manuevers occur in phase I, but this is a very brief period. The carving of the turn lasts much longer than the initiation of the turn but is little discussed by ski technicians in general. This is a shame, because it is of prime importance.

In phase II, the skier must cope with rapidly accelerating skis as they approach and descend the fall line plus a rapidly increasing centrifugal force. Arriving in phase III, the skier enters the most difficult portion of the turn. Mounting compression, centrifugal force and gravitational forces must be absorbed while

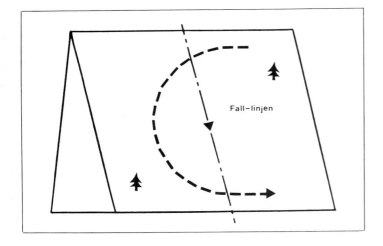

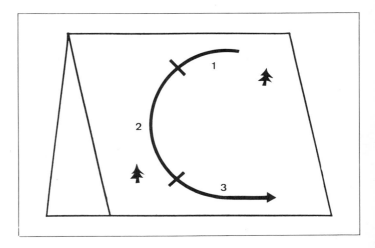

preserving good line and sliding. It should be clear that the difficulties of phase III can be anticipated during phases I and II and that technical faults in the earlier phases will amplify the difficulties already present in phase III.

The fall line is the maximum steepness that the skier will meet when turning across the slope. While traversing to the point where the turn will be started, the skis are directed across the fall line. Consequently, this traverse represents a slope of minimum steepness. Entering the turn, the skis swing more and more parallel to the fall line. As this happens, the skis are pointed down the maximum steepness of the slope, whether they are flat or edged.

The acceleration that results makes this psychologically a difficult part of the turn, no matter if the skier is a World Cup downhiller or a beginner. As the skier returns to a new traverse headed in the op-

1977 Ladies' World Cup Champion
Lichtenstein's Hanni Wenzel in the Maribor giant slalom, 1977.

posite direction (III), the path followed by the skier decreases in pitch as the skis are turned again across the fall line. In reality, every turn crossing the fall line constitutes a passage from a flat to a slope to a flat again, with a resulting compression at the end of the turn which must be absorbed by the skier.

During phase I, centrifugal force helps to press the skis against the hill. Gravity pulls in nearly the opposite direction. The steeper the hill, the greater the possibility that the feet of the skier will be higher on the slope than his center of mass. In all cases, the CM will follow an arc to the inside of the path scribed by the skis due to the body's inward lean to resist the centrifugal force generated by the turn.

Phase II produces an acceleration of the skier as he descends straight down the fall line. Centrifugal force at this time is no longer operating against gravity but at right angles to it. The centrifugal force, balanced by the power of the skier's leg muscles, exerts increasing pressure on the skis. The turn is carefully controlled by angulation and the degree of edge angle of the skis and by steering, with pivoting of the ski increased or checked in order to maintain carving.

During phase III, the skis return across the fall line to a new traverse. The skier undergoes successively: 1.) a compression due to the decreasing steepness as he passes from the fall line to the traverse, 2.) centrifugal force acting in combination with 3.) gravity, pulling the skier down the slope. To avoid being pulled down the hill in a side-slip, the compression must be absorbed with the skis placed on edge to "bite" the snow. The first part of a turn can be likened to turning on a banked surface and the last part to turning on a fall-away.

Every skier has experienced a loss of control during the last part of a turn, whether in relatively easy conditions or on the steep, icy slopes of the expert. All have admired the ability of World Cup racers to hold their skis in a perfect arc close to the slalom gate even on the seemingly vertical ice of international slalom hills. Certainly the equipment, conditioning and motivation of these skiers play important roles, but they also have a technical secret. Their extreme hip angulation tilts the legs to the inside of the turn, placing the skis on maximum edge.

If a course is inspected after a race, it is evident that the rut made by the racers is deepest close to the gate at the end of the turn. Obviously, the forces generated by the turn are greatest toward the end. Here the skis are throwing out the most snow as the skier attempts to hold the line of the course.

A special note for racers and coaches: even on the World Cup it is possible to hear people speak of "accelerating out of a turn". But upon closer examination it becomes evident that this is impossible. There is no acceleration out of a turn at normal racing speed. Inevitably there is a deceleration in phase III, the final phase of a turn. A racer may give an illusion of accelerating out of the turn if he loses as little speed as possible in phase III; the speed that he gained accelerating down the fall-line during phases I and II.

Always on the outside ski!
Ingemar Stenmark, Sweden. 1978 Watrerville Valley GS.

Pole Plant!
Phil Mahre, USA. 1978 World Championship slalom.
Garmisch-Partenkirchen, West Germany.

Downhill racer in suspension.
Herbert Plank, Italy. 1978 downhill, Laax, Switzerland.

Movements must be adapted to the terrain.
Ingemar Stenmark, Sweden.
1977 Are slalom.

Klaus Heidegger, Austria. ►
1978 Kitzbuhel slalom.
Conditions: the steepest section of the course, ice.

This slalom was won by Heidegger. The pictures comprising the sequence were taken by two synchronized cameras positioned in front of and behind the skier. The conditions encountered by the racers here were so difficult that a small technical error in turning would immediately become a major problem. Klaus Heidegger, known for his great physical strength and hard training, is among the best slalom racers in the world. When course conditions are most severe, he can often out-ski his competitors.

Frame 1: As Heidegger unweights, he stands on his outside ski.

Frame 2: Closing the radius of the turn, Heidegger angulates over his outside ski. Notice that his upper body is twisted, facing down the fall line.

Frame 3: Heidegger continues the turn in a wide stance, the flexing of his left ski indicating that it is supporting most of his weight. As he edges across the fall line, Heidegger must resist forces of 300-500 pounds with his outside leg.

Frame 4: Heidegger unweights, losing contact with the snow. The wide-spread arms and pole plant improve his stability.

Frame 5: As he steers his skis around the pole, Heidegger's chest faces the outside of the turn. Again, he weights only his outside ski which flexes under the pressure.

Piero Gros, Italy. 1978 Kitzbuhel slalom.
Conditions: the steepest section of the course, ice.

Well known for his numerous Olympic and World Cup victories, Piero Gros placed fourth in this Hahnenkamm slalom. Here again, the cameras were synchronized. Notice the similarity in technique of Heidegger and Gros, the only significant difference being that Gros skis with his feet much closer together. As a consequence, he must angulate more with his hip to achieve the same degree of edging as Heidegger and, in so doing, runs a greater risk of standing on his inside ski.

Frame 1: Gros weights the heels of his feet with very little forward bend at his ankles.

Frame 2: Gros' edge-set requires extreme hip angulation since his feet are so close together. His balance point has moved forward, over the center of his skis.

Frame 3: As he concludes the first turn on the tails of his skis, Gros uses a strong pole plant to improve his balance.

Frame 4: Gros has brought his feet closer together again and is driving the turn with hip angulation and very little knee angulation.

Frame 5: While preparing for his pole plant, Gros spreads his skis and makes an edge-set with strong angulation of his right knee.

Piero Gros, Italy
1977 Hahnenkamm slalom.

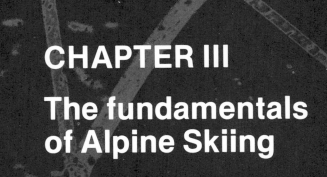

CHAPTER III

The fundamentals of Alpine Skiing

1. Movements of the arms and ski poles

As we have seen earlier, every movement of a part of the body alters the position of the center of mass, which then requires another change to remain in balance. This is precisely why every unnecessary gesture should be avoided.

The most essential arm movement is the pole plant. It should be made with relaxed, extended arms and only a simple wrist movement to bring the tip of the pole forward and into contact with the snow. This is clearly visible in photos taken of World Cup competition.

The best skiers today plant their poles during edge-set and unweighting for added stability during this delicate transition period between the end of one turn and the beginning of the next. Planting the ski pole provides a greater margin of security through better balance for all skiers and allows the racer to strive for better sliding and greater speed.

Phil Mahre, USA: ▶
1978 World Championship Slalom. Garmisch-Partenkirchen.

In extreme situations, the unweighted legs and skis can be swung around a solid pole plant. The lateral pole plant of World Cup racers provides a turning impulse and also assists the change of inward lean and angulation from one turn to another. In addition, the vertical force of the pole plant can play a role in unweighting.

backward stability to the skier during edge-set and unweighting. To momentarily stabilize the upper body, the pole is best planted forward, but to provide pivoting force it must be planted to the side according to the radius of the turn and the terrain.

During an edge-set, the skis decelerate as they bite into the snow, while the upper body continues forward.

Avalement or rebound unweighting techniques are most commonly used when making short radius turns on steep terrain. Here, the forward-backward support of the pole plant is helpful. On flatter terrain with larger turns, where up-unweighting is more often seen, the pole plant becomes less important. The top athletes have such good balance on their skis that they often don't need the assistance of pole plants on these easier slopes and smoother turns. Nevertheless, the arm position and often even the wrist motion are retained, even though the pole is not actually set into the snow.

The pole plant can provide both lateral and forward-

Piero Gros, Italy.
1977 Voss slalom.

A rebound turn is one of the faster movements in skiing but can be made even faster with a good pole plant. Gros applies great pressure to the pole to help him go rapidly from the finish of one turn to an immediate carving of the next. He finished second in this race on a steep slalom hill in Norway.

The pole plant, correctly timed, holds the upper body in position. It can last a relatively long time in order that the unweighted skis and feet can be correctly positioned under the body for driving through the turn.

The most common errors involve timing. If the pole is planted too late, the results can be negative, such as the next turn being delayed. Planting the pole at exactly the right time becomes very difficult, however, if the arms are contracted, stiff or occupied with unnecessary movements or if the skier tries to plant the pole with a large gesture instead of a wrist movement. Furthermore, dropping the hand or arm after planting the pole will create problems for the following turn.

It is generally agreed that modern ski poles, exceptionally lightweight and strong, should come to the bottom of the breast bone when standing on the floor in ski boots. Too short a pole will prevent maximum efficiency from the pole plant and will necessitate large gestures instead of a flick of the wrist.

Toshiro Kaiwa, Japan.
1977 Are slalom.

The slalom expert from Japan is photographed between two tight turns. Thrown into the air by the terrain and his edge-set, Kaiwa plants his pole laterally to stabilize his body while transferring his weight from the inside edge of one ski to the other. The arms are wide and extended to aid balance. By planting the pole laterally, the lever from the pole to Kaiwa's center of mass is very long, providing greater force.

Hans Hinterseer, Austria.
1978 Madonna di Campiglio giant slalom.

Hinterseer's pole plant gives him good balance as he becomes airborn out of a dip between two giant slalom turns. The stability of his upper body allows him to smoothly change his weight from his right to his left ski, turn in the air and angulate for the new turn. If good balance is maintained, it is possible for the skier to improvise using natural features for easier skiing. The arms are always positioned for ultimate balance, therefore the preparation, pole plant and return is done with maximum economy of motion. As in this case, if the planted pole gives a pivoting impulse toward either side, it will last until the skier regains contact with the snow again.

Toshira Kaiwa, Japan.
World Championship Slalom. Garmisch-Partenkirchen, 1978.
   Due to the speed generated in the preceeding turn, Kaiwa must
move the point of the pole forward toward the next turn before planting. Good skiers do this with only a wrist movement.

Peter Aellig, Switzerland.
World Championship Slalom. Garmisch-Partenkirchen, 1978.

Blocking of the upper body by a strong lateral pole plant can most easily be seen from behind. The body is stabilized in all planes in such a way that the unweighted feet and skis are easily pivoted under the torso. This achieves the new inward lean and angulation required to make the next turn.

Christian Neureuther, West Germany. ▶
Crans-Montana slalom, 1979.
Conditions: hard snow and ice.

The first pole plant of this sequence occurs during the skier's unweighting while the second occurs at the same time as a very violent edge-set. Both turns have an exceptionally round radius and the pole plants are, therefore, made to the side of the body. Neureuther's second pole plant slows down his upper body so much that his feet and skis shoot out in front of him.

2. Angulation-anticipation

What makes one skier superior to another is his ability to make a good turn. Skiing with the skis banked onto their edges is absolutely necessary for good turning, traversing and control of line and speed. The best technique for this is angulation, and lack of angulation is the number one pit-fall for all alpine skiers.

The most common and important errors made by most skiers who can handle most slopes are leaning to the inside of their turns (no hip angulation) and skiing on the inside ski or on both skis while turning. Interestingly

enough, both faults are closely related. Without correct angulation, the skier is obliged to press on the inside ski or on both skis. Even knee angulation is of little help. Without hip angulation to bring the skier into balance over the outside ski, the skier weights both skis simultaneously, with accompanying bad balance and poor sliding.

Angulation refers to the fact that two parts of the body are not on the same axis and that the meeting of the axes of the two segments form an angle. In skiing, when the axes of the chest and legs form an angle at the hips, we observe that the skier is "angulated at the hips". This kind of angulation produces the best advantage for balancing on the edges of the skis. It is also the best way for the

In many ways, the forces acting on a bicyclist and a skier are very similar. To resist the centrifugal force of a turn, both the skier and the bicycle rider must lean toward the inside of the turn.

All four images in this photo have practically the same general inclination toward the inside of the turn as drawn from the point of contact with the ground through the center of mass.

A skier turning with his weight concentrated on the inside edge of his outside ski is similar to a bicyclist in that both have very small areas of contact with the ground. The bicyclist remains in balance while leaning in by continually correcting with the handlebars. The skier maintains his line through the turn and his balance on the inside edge of his outside ski by changing his hip and knee angulation and must be able to adjust quickly to compensate for bumps, ice patches, holes and sideslipping.

body to equalize and resist the forces generated in turning. In angulation, the resultant of forces, produced by turning or traversing, acting on the center of mass passes through the outside hip joint to the outside ski. It is a flexion-rotation (bending-twisting) movement of the body which tilts the lower part into the center of the turn or into the hill when traversing, and the upper body out over the outside ski.

Angulation is primarily the result of the work of a group of muscles around the waist and hip which stabilize the upper body over the outside leg. The contraction of this muscle group rotates the entire leg toward the inside of the turn. At the same time, it twists the waist toward the outside leg. Combined with a slight bending

forward at the waist, the hip is moved to the center of the turn and the inside leg is placed slightly ahead of the outside leg.

It is crucial to understand that the skier twists at the waist instead of bending the torso to the side. Tilting the torso would result in stiffness, whereas even in a very angulated position, the hip is free to flex and extend for balance and shock absorption.

The role of the knee and hip of the inside leg is minor, compared to the work of the outside leg which supports the weight of the body and the forces generated by the turn.

The constant up and down motion of a good skier is not just an attempt to avoid being "static" while turning. It is usually the result of several technical elements. First, it can result from an effort to maintain contact with the

Fausto Radici, Italy.
1978 Kitzbuhel slalom.
Conditions: the steepest section of the course, ice.

This difficult passage requires a round line and Radici needs many well-coordinated technical elements to ski it well. Most important is the ability to finish one turn and begin the next very quickly. The icy, steep slope and tight turns allow him little space between turns.

How does Radici change his inward lean (drawn from the point of support through the approximate center of mass) so radically (65° in 2/10 of a second)? The movement is dramatic because he steps cleanly from one foot to the other with a wide stance. The carving downhill ski provides a platform from which the skier can move, employing all of his muscle power. Stepping these turns from one inside edge to the other is executed with no waste of time or line while giving security, particularly in difficult conditions.

Bruno Confortola, Italy.
1977 Åre giant slalom.
Conditions: transformed ''spring'' snow, artificially hardened.

Primarily a giant slalom specialist, this young Italian also won the combined Europa Cup. So much of good skiing is dependent on correct edging, and in this turn Confortola employs perfect hip and knee angulation over bumpy terrain. A static position is to be avoided at all costs, particularly in mogulled terrain. In the first two pictures, Confortola is edging with knee and hip angulation combined, but in preparing to absorb the bump coming up, he extends the downhill leg which naturally reduces the knee angulation. In the last picture, the right leg is very bent to absorb the bump. This makes knee angulation possible again. Hip angulation often diminishes toward the end of a long turn as the skier returns to a position square over his skis.

Uli Spiess, Austria.
1978 Laax Downhill.
Conditions: melting spring snow.

Young Austrian Uli Spiess, en route to his first World Cup victory, shows an ability to adjust his angulation. Seen from behind, the way he increases his angulation over his right ski is unmistakable. In the first picture, he banks into the hill. He then increases pressure on the outside ski by moving his waist to the left, whereas in the first picture the hips appear to be over the right ski.

snow through bumps and holes, alternately absorbing and extending over the bumps. But a racer is often crouched low by the gate and more or less extended between the turns. However, if the turns are rutted, exactly the opposite timing would be used: straightening to press the skis into the rut by the gate and compressing to absorb the bump as the skier comes out of the rut.

The constant up and down motion of a good skier is not just an attempt to avoid being "static" while turning. It is usually the result of several technical elements. First, it can result from an effort to maintain the skis in contact with the snow through bumps and holes, alternately absorbing and extending over the bumps. A racer skiing a rutted course will straighten to press the skis into the rut by the gate and then compress to absorb the bump as the

Josef Walcher, Austria.
1978 Laax Downhill.
Conditions: melting spring snow.

The current World Downhill Champion is pictured on his way to posting the best intermediate time in the 1978 World Cup downhill in Laax, Switzerland. Through this high-speed turn he counteracts the centrifugal force by standing only on his outside ski. A balanced combination of inward "bicycle lean" and hip angulation allow him to maintain pressure on his outside ski.

skis climb out of the back of the rut. On a smooth course, however, a racer will use the opposite timing: crouched low by the gate and more or less extended between the turns. This constant flexing must, therefore, serve another purpose.

From a functional standpoint, a joint that is very bent has more freedom for twisting movements (eg. the angulation-anticipation movements so common in ski racing) than a joint in a straighter, stiffer position. The up and down motion, then, assists angulation. To progressively increase angulation from the beginning to the end of a turn, the good skier smoothly bends more and more in the ankles, knees, hips and back. At the end of the turn, maximum angulation, maximum flexion and maximum weighting of the skis occur simultaneously.

An extremely angulated position is very stable, since the skier's center of mass is low, but it also has intrinsic disadvantages. If the skier were to try to remain in this low position, the contraction of the muscles would result in stiffness and more fatigue. During training the best skiers constantly search for the posture on their skis giving optimum balance and greatest relaxation. Although forced to move from this position by the turns, terrain or other forces, they return to this efficient neutral stance wherever possible. This explains the straightening between turns, a position allowing more relaxed, less fatiguing free-skiing.

Timing is an essential feature of proper angulation. For the movement to be effective, it should be performed as smoothly as possible. The hip must be angulated from the beginning of the turn, but angulation will be progressively increased until the edge-set. The edge-set at the end of the turn is an integral part of angulation. At this point the skier may or may not make a sudden movement of knee angulation, but will always set the edges, providing a platform for him to launch his feet and skis into the next turn. A good skier may start a new turn by carrying the return movement (from angulation to a

Ingrid Eberle, Austria.
1978 Crans-Montana slalom.

Lea Soelkner, Austria.
1978 Crans-Montana slalom.

Lea Soelkner, Austria.

Lisa-Marie Morerod, Switzerland.

Hip angulation is one of skiing's most difficult movements to learn and perform correctly. We have searched for over two years to find the right camera angles which reveal the nature of this movement.

Lea Soelkner, the slalom World Champion, is compared in the same gate to one of her teammates, Ingrid Eberle, at the moment when the skiers brush past the pole. Lise Marie Morerod is also shown for comparison.

Angulation of the hip is the most effective way to edge the skis, particularly on ice or steep slopes. In these pictures, two important characteristics of angulation are evident: the twisting of the hip toward the inside of the turn and the pivoting of the upper body toward the outside of the turn.

When viewed both from behind and in front, the twisting of the skier's body (moving the hip in and the upper body out) is easily separated from the other movements. In the photo-composition to the lower right, Ingrid Eberle's shoulders are aligned to illustrate how the chest does not change orientation as the feet are turned around the slalom pole. Morerod is photographed passing the same gate (photo, upper right). The different directions in which her chest and skis are facing are indicated by arrows. This is often referred to as a "counter-rotation" of the upper body.

In the photo upper left, the angle at Soelkner's waist is formed by lines representing her upper and lower body. Notice how she is in perfect balance over her outside ski with her left ski lifted off the snow. The skis are carving well without the slightest angulation of the knee. This is classic World Cup ski technique.

Ingrid Eberle, Austria.

more centered stance) directly through to a new angulation. Shifting the weight to the opposite leg changes the angulation and the "bicycle lean" of the body in the new turn. If this were to be done only from the waist up, it would be slower and would require more energy to complete the turn.

Gustavo Thoeni, Italy.
1978 Madonna di Campiglio slalom.
Conditions: very steep slope, newly falling snow over ice.

This sequence of the former World Cup Champion demonstrates typical timing of angulation.

In the photos top left and right, Thoeni uses exclusively hip angulation to turn. Notice too, that he has twisted his upper body to face down the fall line.

In the photo to the lower left, taken one-tenth of a second later, Thoeni's hip angulation has been dramatically overtaken by knee angulation. His hip angulation diminishes as Thoeni's upper body becomes more "square", facing the direction of his skis.

In the lower right photo, Thoeni has unweighted with a pole plant. In this series, Thoeni's hip angulation coincides with his driving of the turn, his knee movement with the edge-set, and his unweighting with the beginning of the next turn.

Consequently, angulation is an essential element in the starting, balance and driving of turns by the modern skier, the correct proportion of hip and knee angulation at every moment of the turn being the secret to finesse in good skiing.

Maria Epple, West Germany.
1978 Megeve giant slalom.
Conditions: soft snow.

This young girl became giant slalom World Champion at Garmisch-Partenkirchen in 1978. The photomontage catches Maria Epple long before she crosses in front of the gate to the left of the picture.

To insure that her skis will be carving all of the way around, she has angulated from the very start of the turn. By angulating at the waist, her right leg is free to drive the outside ski through the turn. Most important, her chest continues to face down the fall line, instead of rotating with her skis as they turn. By *not* rotating, she is able to keep her hip inside the arc of the turn and remain angulated with her weight on the outside ski.

Ingemar Stenmark, Sweden.
1978 Crans-Montana slalom.

In this relatively long radius turn Stenmark uses angulation of the hip which is most pronounced as he passes the gate. The snow is hard, but not ice. Throughout the turn he doesn't use knee angulation to make the skis carve on the grippy snow.

The importance of twisting the upper body in relation to the pivoting skis to achieve hip angulation is obvious. Ingemar's skiing is very smooth in spite of the rapidity of his movements.

In the separate pictures, Stenmark also demonstrates ideal position. The other skiers differ from him in that they all exaggerate some element: more on the inside ski, more bent over at the waist, harsher on the edges, more pronounced knee angulation, more contracted, poor forward-backward balance, and greater inward lean of the shoulders. Stenmark won this race by a large margin.

Fabienne Serrat, France.
1978 Arosa giant slalom.
Conditions: soft snow.

The high speed and terrain features of this difficult turn resulted in extreme forces which had to be powerfully resisted by the skiers if the proper line were to be maintained. In this situation, the edging is exclusively by hip angulation because a flexed or angulated knee wouldn't be strong enough to withstand the pressure. The forces generated by the turn have caused Serrat's right ankle to roll out in the first picture of the sequence, but toward the end of the turn, she stiffens her ankle joint and increases her edging.

Lise-Marie Morerod, Switzerland.
1978 Crans-Montana slalom.
Conditions: Ice.

The twisting-bending at the waist of top skiers like Lise-Marie Morerod, which places the upper body out over the outside ski, is very evident when viewed from above. Even as she pivots her skis around the pole, Morerod's upper body hardly changes direction. Skiing that is so clean of unnecessary movements becomes graceful as well as athletic.

Anticipation

Anticipation is a very efficient turning force where a skier "anticipates" a turn by propelling his upper body into the turn before his skis have started to change direction. It is a rotation movement of the body in the direction of the new turn as the skis are pivoted across the fall line during the edge-set that ends the previous turn. At this instant, the body is twisted around the waist with the feet and legs pivoted in nearly opposite directions as the chest. But when the skis are unweighted, the skier "unwinds", and the skis straighten out, swinging back underneath the body which is usually stabilized by a solid pole plant.

Angulation and anticipation are very closely related gestures. Angulation, a double twisting of the legs and hips, and anticipation, a twisting of the upper body, are often combined into one global movement. As the skis

are checked during the edge-set ending one turn, the mass of the upper body continues to move downhill toward the following turn, providing the impulse for its initiation.

3. Unweighting

Speed of movement has become very important in World Cup skiing in recent years. One factor has been equipment: better fitting, more efficient ski boots with very stiff lateral characteristics and skis with carving capacity that almost catapult the skier out of a turn. These skis, especially when made of a "hot" material like fiberglass, can produce the same effect as a polevaulter changing to a fiberglass pole for the first time.

Modern equipment has had a profound influence on unweighting techniques. The completion and beginning of short radius turns requires speed, but with higher speed turns of a longer radius, keeping the skis on the snow and avoiding excessive unweighting becomes a problem. In effect, the skillful skier modifies

his unweighting techniques to correspond to the conditions, instinctively choosing from among the different elements in his or her technique.

Turn initiation usually requires that the skis be unweighted so that they can pass freely underneath the skier, from one side to another. World Cup racers use a variety of manuevers to accomplish this and the kind of unweighting they use depends on their speed, the steepness of the slope, the presence or absence of bumps or holes, and the size of the turn to be made.

Terrain features are often used to unweight the skis, but historically unweighting techniques have been described as either downunweighting or upunweighting. In recent years, however, the best skiers in the world, and particularly the coming stars Andreas

Wenzel, Paul Frommelt, Phil Mahre, Ingemar Stenmark and Christian Orlainsky, have perfected an unweighting technique originally introduced to World Cup racing by Patrick Russell, Gustavo Thoeni and Piero Gros. Combined with either an up or down movement, they push their feet forward, giving the impression that they are

Gustavo Thoeni, Italy.
1977 Are slalom

There are many different forms of unweighting and the best skiers are not limited to using only one unweighting technique. By varying their unweighting, they are able to totally adapt their skiing to the terrain. Here, Thoeni flexes as he passes by the gate with a down-unweighting motion, but fractions of a second later he extends to remain in contact with the snow after passing over the bump.

sitting slightly back. Pushing first one foot and then the other into the traverse at the end of a turn can also be combined with a lateral step to dynamically transfer their weight from one ski to the other.

Upunweighting - Upunweighting is produced by pushing the hips, and therefore the center of mass, upwards. The upward acceleration of the center of mass overcomes gravity and a momentary weightlessness results.

The extensor muscle groups of the ankles, knees and hips are all involved and in extreme upunweighting by vigorous skiers, an extension of all these joints, including the back, can be seen. Such an unweighting by extension is often "prepared" by a down-motion, either a result of the angulation at the edge-set or simply to give the following up-motion greater amplitude.

As the body is pushed up from a more or less bent

Ingemar Stenmark, Sweden.
1977 Bormio giant slalom.

Here Stenmark uses a down motion to absorb a large bump while unweighting his skis to initiate a turn. His stomach muscles draw his knees up and his chest forward over the bump.

In the second picture of the sequence, he is completely extended to maintain contact with the snow. Two tenths of a second later, he makes an extreme downunweighting motion, because of the terrain, to start a high speed turn. What is most impressive is the independence of Stenmark's leg action which allows him to simultaneously transfer from one inside edge to the other.

position, the skis are first pressed into the snow and then unweighted. If the upward push of the legs is also directed forward, an acceleration can occur, although in soft snow this forward motion can hinder the gliding of the skis.

Thrusting the feet forward - This movement of the lower legs and feet forward combines two often opposing effects on the skis. Modern skis can accelerate in relation to the skier while at the same time biting and carving better as their tails are progressively weighted. With the feet slightly ahead of the center of mass, the skier can also better absorb the compression and braking which occur during the final phase of the turn. The skier anticipates, with his feet, the checking by the edge-set, while at the same time allowing his knees and hips to absorb the pressure by letting the feet be pushed upward. If the feet were directly under the body, the stiffness of the boots would prevent the ankles from flexing.

World Cup racers always cultivate great independence in the movements of their legs and feet. Rarely does the forward push of both feet happen at the same time. Instead, the outside foot is first thrust forward, the weight transferred to the inside foot which is then steered and pushed into the next turn. Such a sequence of movements allows a rapid change of angulation so that the inside ski can be set very quickly onto its inside edge.

Downunweighting - is a sudden vertical drop of the hips, and therefore the center of mass, which produces momentary weightlessness. The drop is produced by the skier bending low; ideally flexing at the waist, knees and ankle joints equally. The movement can be produced either by relaxing the extensor muscles that hold the body erect or by contracting the flexor muscles to accelerate the downward movement and even pull the skis and feet up off of the snow.

In either case, the extensor muscles must then contract to slow and stop the down motion. If the movement is blocked on a pole plant and edge-set, the

Phil Mahre, USA.
1977 Sun Valley slalom.

Mahre uses an avalement unweighting to link two very round turns. Avalement unweighting is ideal for absorbing the rebound of the skis following an edge set.

In the first and last pictures of the sequence, the angulation is extreme. By the third picture, the left knee and hip joints have straightened to keep the outside ski carving and in contact with the snow.

A forward thrust of the feet, an important component of avalement, is very evident. Bending forward at the waist as the feet are pushed forward, as in the second photo, is not as apparent in the second generation of World Cup skiers, like Mahre, as it was in the skiing of racers like Patrick Russel who originated the avalement technique.

resulting extension is much the same as the rebound of a bouncing rubber ball, aided by the spring of the skis as they return from reverse camber.

Contraction of the extensor muscles of the legs to slow down and stop the down-motion in all variations of downunweighting is a preparation for the extension of the legs that must follow if the skier is to return to a relaxed position over his skis. All downunweighting, whether by avalement, rebound or simply relaxing the extensor muscles, is followed by an extension of the outside leg in the new turn to maintain contact with the snow.

The low body position that downunweighting produces has several interesting features. Since the

Andreas Wenzel, Lichtenstein.
1977 Are slalom.

A rebound turn is of use when a skier wishes to obtain complete control in a few fractions of a second. Lively, good carving skis are an important aid in this technique.

Rebound is the result of an extremely vigorous flexion-extension motion producing an effect much like a rubber ball. In the first picture of the photomontage on the facing page, Wenzel has a very high posture, but then drops abruptly. In the second image (also shown above), he sets his edges rapidly and energetically at the same time as he halts the down motion (which stretches the extensor muscles) and pushes upward with his legs. For this reason, he is then catapulted into the air and can position his skis quickly for the next turn.

center of mass is lower, there is greater stability. The flexing of the ankles, knees and hip makes greater lateral rotation of the legs possible, which makes knee angulation and foot steering easier.

Lateral Step - World Cup racers make common use of a lateral step between turns to give them a higher line for the following gate. The higher line gives them more time and distance to make the turn and this usually means they can make a longer turn with a greater radius and less braking, consequently greater speed.

A lateral step is made from a traverse or the bottom of the preceeding turn. The outside leg is flexed, then powerfully straightened, thrusting the skier up the hill. As the skier pushes hard on his outside ski it bites into the snow, giving a firmer edge-set at the end of a turn. This thrust can also be directed forward, in which case a slight acceleration results.

It is simple to combine a lateral step with a forward thrust of the feet. The dynamic attack of the best skiers is the result of these movements, often disguising their "velvet-gloved" soft contact with the snow.

The flexion-extension of the outside leg in so many of the photos in this book is very different from two other kinds of transfer steps also taught in skiing: a progressive weighting of the inside ski and the skating step. In World Cup skiing the skiers weight their outside ski throughout the turn, and Ingemar Stenmark is one of the very best at keeping himself balanced over his outside ski. At the end of the turn the best skiers set the inside edge of their outside ski, often lifting their inside ski before pushing over. There clearly is not a progressive weighting of the inside ski. With a lateral step the skier is immediately prepared for the next turn as he steps from a finished turn to a ski that is flat or even already edged for the following turn.

The lateral step has another advantage over skating or finishing a turn on the inside ski. With the latter two, the upper body must move forward radically to keep the inside ski turning and remain in balance. But in the lateral step the skier always remains over his skis, sim-

◄

Ingemar Stenmark, Sweden.
1977 Solynieve giant slalom.

Between two very low and angulated positions in the beginning and at the end of this photomontage, Stenmark unweights by extension with a lateral step. The rise and fall of his center of mass is propelled by the power of his legs. Stenmark's weight is totally transferred from one ski to the other as he steps from a very edged outside ski to a flat inside ski.

The thrusting of the legs, common to both up-unweighting and lateral stepping, can be efficient when these two elements are combined as they often are in World Cup ski technique.

Ingemar Stenmark, Sweden.
1977 Sun Valley giant slalom.
Conditions: hard, man-made snow.

Ingemar performs a lateral step. With no unnecessary movements he transfers his weight *totally* from one ski to the other. Notice that he easily combines a lateral step with a thrusting of the feet forward.

ply moving sideways from the outside ski to the inside ski. This element of unweighting allows the skier to remain in good balance over the skis and in good contact with the snow.

Once the step has been completed, the hip is not in a high position, even though the outside leg is very extended, allowing the following turn to be angulated very efficiently. It should be emphasized, however, that there should be a total weight transfer from one ski to the other. Failure to transfer the weight fully robs the movement of its dynamic quality and necessitates a series of corrective gestures to remain in balancee and on line. The lateral step is a dynamic, powerful movement that should always be smoothly executed so that the free sliding of the skis will not be disturbed.

The manner of unweighting which will be performed by the skier is selected instinctively. Good skiers unweight according to their speed, the terrain, and the radius of the turn. Obviously, the unweighting techniques used at slow speed are different from those used at higher speed or on bumpy terrain. The virtuoso skier judges by feel what is best for optimum sliding of the skis, control and line. This instinct comes first from the athletic capacities of the skier, but just as much from the training and coaching he has received.

Irene Epple, West Germany.
1979 Les Gets giant slalom.
Conditions: Steep terrain with hard-packed snow.

Irene Epple, one of the top giant slalom specialists of the 1979 womens' World Cup, skis the most difficult part of one of the steepest giant slaloms of the World Cup circuit. Her movements, as shown here, can be considered typical of the best giant slalom skiing of today.

In the first picture of the photomontage, Epple makes her edge-set while extremely well balanced over her downhill ski. Such good balance permits her subsequent extension to be relaxed and efficient. From her extended body position, she then angulates as quickly as possible with her hip. This is the "anti-rotation"

movement which prevents her upper body from turning with her skis, and is more accentuated in womens' skiing than in mens'. Skiers who have mastered this technical element at this moment of the turn are rarely seen over-rotating with the chest.

Irene's movements through the remainder of the turn are classical, a carving of the turn with the inside ski lifted and the weight centered on the middle of the outside ski.

Monika Kaserer, Austria.
1977 Sun Valley slalom.

Monika Kaserer, winner of numerous World Cup and FIS medals during her long career, rebounds off her edges to initiate a short radius turn. The rebound from the severe edge-set in the first picture of the sequence has unweighted her skis and she extends her legs to regain contact with the snow.

Kaserer's pole plant is so powerful that the pole momentarily flexes. The pole plant stabilizes and supports her as her skis are rebounding. A proper pole plant can be an integral part of an unweighting by rebound.

Perrine Pelen, France.
1977 St. Gervais slalom.

This photomontage captures Pelen skiing to one of her many
World Cup victories. In order to maintain maximum sliding, she
angulates and pushes off her downhill ski. Pelen pushes herself up
and over her left ski and then completes the movement by extending
her left leg into an unweighting. She thrusts her feet forward in order to maintain every bit of speed and better ski-snow contact.

Ingemar Stenmark, Sweden (upper sequence).
Anne Marie Moser-Proell, Austria (lower sequence).
1978 Arosa parallel slalom.

Both Stenmark, shown in the photomontage above and Moser-Proell, shown below, approach the end of the turn balanced on their outside skis. At the completion of the turn, as they transfer their weight to their left skis, they thrust their right feet forward. In the 3rd and 4th pictures of the sequence of Stenmark, he moves his right foot from a position behind to a position in front of his left foot. Moser-Proell performs the same movement in the second photo of the sequence below: her right foot advances from a position behind her left foot to a position parallel with her left foot in the 3rd photo.

Becky Dorsey, USA.
1978 Waterville Valley giant slalom.
Conditions: cold, very hard snow.

The lateral step can be used to gain a better line between gates, thereby allowing better gliding and greater acceleration. By stepping out of the turn above, Dorsey raises her line by roughly one meter. This allows her to make a longer, smoother turn with better sliding. Her exceptionally powerful and wide step also enables her to quickly achieve the necessary "bicycle lean" for the following turn.

Heini Hemmi, Switzerland.
1977 Solynieve parallel slalom.

In spite of a wide lateral step, the Olympic Champion's upper body is completely stable and practically motionless.

Ingemar Stenmark, Sweden.
1978 World Cup Final parallel slalom. Arosa.

All of Stenmark's movements are adapted to the terrain and his speed. In the second and third pictures of the sequence above, Stenmark's outside foot is thrust forward as he absorbs the bump. But when he regains contact with the snow in the last frame, he once again is in perfect forward-backward balance over his skis. It is astonishing that a skier can have such perfect balance over this

rough and changing terrain, with its ruts and bumps, while being air-born for so long. A deep down motion followed by an extension of the legs is clearly visible in this sequence.

Ingemar Stenmark, Sweden.
1977 Voss slalom.

Three different unweighting elements are used by Stenmark in linking the four consecutive turns of this sequence. We see unweighting with accent on feet-forward, extension and then avalement. But in all of the turns extremely quiet and stable upper body action is achieved. Ingemar unweights differently to adapt to the various characteristics of each turn: the moderate radius of the first turn, the tight second swing, the hollow between the second and third turns and then the steep slope of the last turn. Stenmark uses low avalement in the last turn to pivot the skis, then weights immediately his right ski, angulating for control on this steep terrain.

World Cup Stem.
Becky Dorsey, USA. Stratton Mountain slalom, 1978.

Lake Placid Giant Slalom ▶
Upper sequence: Ingemar Stenmark, Sweden.
Lower sequence: Peter Luscher, Switzerland.

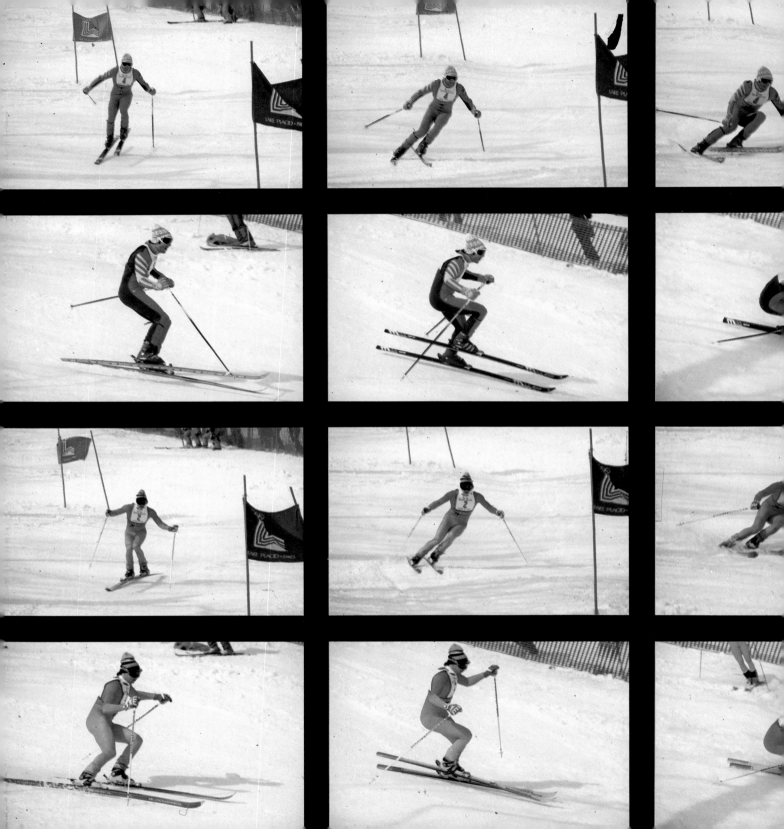

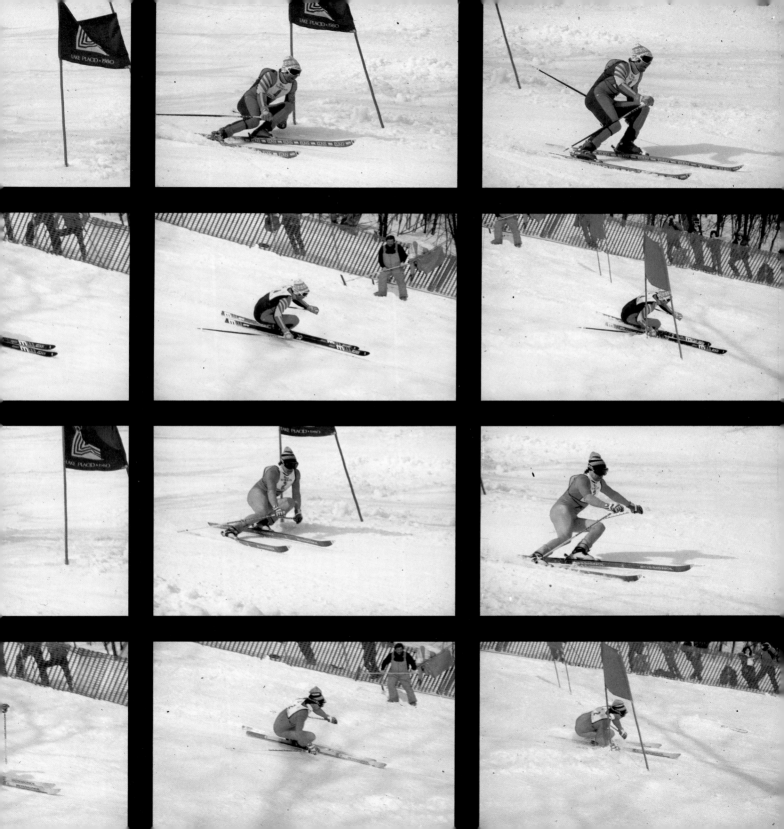

4. Turning

Everyone who wants to ski better envies the control of the good skier. With him, such faults as leaning into the hill, standing on the inside ski or crossing the tips or tails of the skis are rare occurences. The good skier has the same control on steep hills as on flatter slopes, and when turning down a piste, seems to have taken care of all of the balance problems, as he always stands in the center of his skis. Finally, it all seems to be so effortless and easy.

The principle reason for this is that the good skier takes advantage of the turning potential of his skis and feet, instead of a much more tiring swing of the upper body, to direct and control his skis. There is a fundamental difference between using the entire body to turn the skis and merely standing on the skis, weighting them in such a way that they will turn by themselves. Modern skis are made to turn, either when carving or sideslipping. Of course good skiing also uses the turning force of the muscles, first to pivot the skis toward the fall line and then to control the turning of the skis through the remainder of the turn.

Turn initiation and turn completion are distinctly different, each producing unique problems of timing and technique. Most of ski technique is concerned with turn initiation, but turn completion lasts much longer and is more important for good balance and control. Nevertheless, the two are closely related. An error in the beginning of a turn will generally result in difficulties which must be contended with through the remainder of the turn.

Paul Frommelt, the slalom specialist from Lichtenstein, is highly regarded for his ability to make short, round, exact turns down steep, icy slopes. He is able to do this because he makes full use of both the "active"

and the "passive" turning forces of his muscles and skis. He can, therefore, concentrate on his line, remain relaxed, and be smooth, both in starting and in driving his turns. It is this characteristic of his technique, as well as his short but round line, that enabled him to attack and win a medal in the 1978 World Championship slalom, a very steep icy course.

What is the difference between "active" and "passive" turning? Active turning implies the direct use of muscle power to start the skis turning and control the pivoting of the skis throughout the turn. "Passive" turning of the skis is the tendency of all skis to turn whether carving or sideslipping due to their shape, quality and character. The turning aptitudes of the skis are used as much as possible. The edging of the skis, angulation of the skier and the change of angulation between turns all play important roles.

Active turning forces are not exclusively for the young, well-trained athletes, although in these skiers such actions are readily evident; sometimes spec-

The best ski alike!
Upper sequence: Ingemar Stenmark, Sweden. 1979 Are slalom.
Lower sequence: Christian Orlainsky, Austria. 1979 Are slalom.

tacularly so. Every skier at every level uses muscles to turn in an instinctive way; steering of the feet, twisting the upper and lower body around the waist, anticipation, or even a pole plant which blocks the upper body.

The most important *active turning forces* are produced by the rotator muscles located around the waist and acting on the legs or upper body. Every skier in reasonable physical condition can generate a great deal of force with this muscle group. This available power also has the advantage of being completely internal, and therefore can be used without extra preparatory movements, even while airborne. With certain techniques, a turning impulse can be applied to the skis over a long time period, instead of just during the fractions of a second when starting a turn. It should be remembered that these muscles act on bones that

have a great freedom of movement in their joints. When a leg rotator muscle contracts, turning and twisting the leg to the inside or outside, it will pull the hip in the opposite direction. This explains the difference between steering the outside ski with both skis in contact with the snow (where the hip is blocked by the inside ski) and with the inside ski lifted (the waist automatically twisting toward the outside of the turn). When the photomontages are carefully compared, hip angulation is immediately seen as the outside foot is steered. Klaus Heidegger, who lifts his inside ski, demonstrates this often during World Cup races. When steering both legs at the same time, the best skiers naturally retain a very independent action of the legs. During a steering of a turn, the inside leg is twisted away from the body as the outside leg is banked and twisted toward the inside; only the ski that needs to be pivoted is turned.

Every spectator at a World Cup competition has observed a racer, arriving at a gate a little late and off his line, suddenly twist his upper body away from the pole

and wrench his skis into a turn. Both legs have been rotated and the same muscles have pulled the upper body in the opposite direction. It is a dynamic movement that is necessarily short and quick. It can be used by every skier to swing the skis quickly across the fall line, gaining control and applying pressure to the edges. Often referred to as "vissage", this gesture always results in strong angulation of the hip, making the edges bite again. For the competition skier, it may keep him in the course even though he is late and off his line.

Anticipation, with the upper body facing the next turn as the skis swing across the fall line, can also be an important turning force at the beginning of a new turn prepared by an edge-set and unweighting. When the chest is turned down the fall line, with the feet turned across the fall line, the muscles of the back and waist are stretched. When the skis are freed, upon unweighting, the upper and lower body untwist toward each other. If the upper body is blocked with a solid pole plant, all of the turning force is transferred to the

legs. In any case, the upper body, with its greater mass and inertia, will tend to turn less than the legs. This turning mechanism is particularly useful on steeper terrain.

The most important *passive turning forces* come directly from the skis and are a result of the shape, structure and stiffness of the skis, which in turn determines the differences between beginner's and competition models, slalom and downhill skis, and special snow and combination models. Before choosing skis it should be clear what turning characteristics are sought by the buyer and ski manufacturer. Although all skis are designed to make both sideslipping and carving turns, some models are more effective for sideslipping turns and some are more effective for carved turns. This is the principle distinction between skis made for novice skiers and for ski racers respectively.

Sideslipping turns - Because the tip is the widest part of a ski, it creates more friction when it is laid on the snow than the narrower tail section. If it is already sideslipping, even slightly, it will continue to pivot as the tail slides out. This sideslipped pivoting can be controlled to make a turn.

The skier immediately discovers how important his forward-backward balance becomes, since during the turn his skis may suddenly understeer or oversteer instead of skidding along the desired arc. If more pressure is placed on the tip of the ski, the turn will tighten. Likewise, if pressure is applied to the tail of the ski, the turn will straighten. The skier must move immediately to adjust and, in reality, the entire turn is made of countless minute corrections in fore-aft balance. The World Cup skier will commonly push or pull his supporting foot back and forth underneath him in order to quickly shift weight and pressure to the tips or tails as needed.

Carving turns - The side-cut of a ski, its torsional rigidity, sharp edges and reverse camber all help to make a carving ski turn when the edges are pressed into the snow. If the ski is rolled onto its inside edge, with the skier's weight balanced on it, it will carve a turn with the tip and tail following the same line and with a minimum of sideslipping. In a full stop, the skis are pivoted abruptly *across* the direction of travel, resulting in maximum braking.

Just how tight a turn a ski will make while carving depends upon the amount it is banked (ie. the degree of angulation), how much the ski has twisted torsionally, the amount of pressure that is put on the ski to bend it into a "reverse camber" and finally the sidecut. The resulting arc of the ski in contact with the snow will determine the radius of the turn.

Angulation can also be used to close or open a turn by adjusting the edging and therefore the carving potential of the skis. Either knee or hip angulation can be used to edge or flatten a turning ski. The World Cup downhiller uses this technique to hold his line in spite of bumps, compressions, fall-away slopes and high speeds.

Ingemar Stenmark, Sweden. ▶
1979 Oslo slalom.
Conditions: gentle slope with hard-packed snow.

A correctly adapted forward-backward position will allow the skier to achieve the most performance out of his skis and his own strength. Maximum quickness, maximum power and optimum balance are all very related. To move dynamically, the skier must have a solid platform to push off of. This is best provided by a carving ski, and modern skis carve best when they are correctly weighted over their entire length. Good balance is also requisite for quickness because all of a skier's power can then be used for moving dynamically. Skiers in balance can concentrate all of their power for a movement. The out of balance skier must divide his strength between the desired movement and an effort to prevent falling, often resulting in parasite movements and additional fatigue. An out of balance skier will contract more muscles and be slower and stiffer, which results in difficulties in adapting to the terrain. To complete the circle, poor terrain absorbtion will hinder the carving of the skis.

The photomontages to the right and on pages 122-123 were taken nearly simultaneously from in front of and directly to the side of Ingemar Stenmark during his winning second run of the 1979 World Cup slalom at Oslo, Norway. They show a skier whose skis are carving and who is powerful, quick and relaxed; the result of good balance throughout the turn.

Paul Frommelt
1978 World Championship Slalom.

Linking turns

The amount that the skis are pivoted while linking turns is critical and it is precisely at the beginning of a turn that the degree of pivoting must be calculated if the turn is to be executed with a minimum of sideslipping. Numerous body mechanisms exist for pivoting the skis, and all of these mechanisms are more effective when the skis are unweighted.

Fabienne Serrat, France. Pfronten slalom, 1979 (upper sequence). **Regina Sackl**, Austria. 1979 Pfronten slalom. (lower sequence). Conditions: a transition from a flat to a steep slope. Hard snow.

After a smooth edge-set, Serrat pivots both skis simultaneously while unweighted. Regina Sackl pivots her skis independently after a longer edge-set.

Both skiers pass the inside gate, in the first frame of the sequences, with their bodies facing the same direction, but they quickly differentiate themselves in their next movements. By the second frame, Serrat is unweighted and already pivoting her skis into the next turn, but Sackl is still on her edges. However, where Sackl completely pivots her skis into the following turn in only one frame,

Serrat pivots her skis through two frames. Sackl has used the faster pivoting action of foot steering and rebound-producing edge-set, with each foot acting independently. Fabienne Serrat's edge-set has also given her a rebound unweighting, but she requires more time to complete the turning of her skis.

Where does Serrat's pivoting come from ? She has used a mechanism different from the independent foot steering of Sackl. Between the last two frames of the sequence, Serrat has moved her hip toward the inside of the new turn (hip angulation), but of course this cannot be accomplished without a twisting of the hip joints. The twisting of her hips toward the gate produces an opposite pivoting of her legs, turning the skis. Finishing one turn and starting the next by going from one perfectly angulated position to another has allowed her to pivot her skis without slowing down.

The possibility of using pivoting forces generated entirely within the skier, by muscular work against the inertia of the skier's own body mass, is one of the secrets of finesse in skiing. It is used all of the time by all of the World Cup elite, albeit unconsciously. It is difficult to pick out, nevertheless biomechanically sound.

Cindy Nelson, USA.
1978 Crans-Montana slalom.
Conditions: gates set on a side-hill.

In the frames at the far left of this sequence, Cindy stands directly over her feet. From the third to the fourth frames she uses progressively more heel thrust, weighting the back half of her skis. In the last picture, Cindy has pivoted her outside ski sharply around the pole and places it very much on edge.

Cindy has pushed her feet far ahead of her in this sequence to prepare for the braking of her skis caused by the hard edge-set. This action allowed her to position her feet to resist the momentum of her upper body mass as the centrifugal force generated by the very tight turn attempts to throw her out of balance.

Ingemar Stenmark, Sweden.
1979 Oslo slalom.

· The inset photos show Stenmark, the fastest skier in this run, and Franz Gruber, who finished 4th, at precisely the instant of their edge-set and pole plant.

A skier's posture must allow him the full use of his power in order to achieve maximum quickness. A position properly balanced over his skis will also allow him to be more relaxed. Notice how Stenmark's posture allows his muscles much more efficient working angles than Gruber's.

A more precise definition of forward-backward weighting (or leverage) should be given. There is a big difference between weighting the toes or heels of the foot inside the ski boot and positions of forward or backward weighting of the tips or tails of the skis. In the first instance the point of maximum pressure is adjusted from roughly the center of the ski boot to a point underneath the toe piece of the ski binding when moving forward or underneath the heel piece in a backward movement. This can be accomplished with extremely subtle movements of the foot underneath the body or even by flexing specific muscles in the foot and calf.

In the second instance there is a global movement of the body to a "forward" or "backward" position with all of the balance problems that such movements entail. With modern skis, specifically designed for carving turns, moving the pressure point under the foot is enough to radically alter the radius of the carved turn, either opening it up or making it tighter. On the other hand, positions over the tips or tails do not have a good influence on the carving or control of the skis. Pressure on the tip will not increase its grip on the snow, but will certainly make the tail of the ski start to slip. This will happen until the pressure is brought back under the foot again. A position in the opposite direction will release the pressure on the tip while the tail bites more and more, resulting in a straightening of the turn.

Backweighting frees the tips of pressure so that they can subsequently absorb the roughness of the snow and terrain as smoothly as possible. If, instead, the tips are heavily weighted by a forward position of the body, the elasticity of the ski is mostly taken up and it will strike harshly against terrain irregularities instead of absorb the roughness of the piste, thereby resulting in greater friction and poorer sliding. Further, the extra muscular work necessary to support a position that is, in reality, out of balance forward makes relaxed skiing impossible and the sliding freedom of the skis is correspondingly restricted.

A well constructed ski transmits the weight of the skier over the entire area of the ski in contact with the snow as evenly as possible when the skier is in balance over the center of his foot. This is of little importance on ice, where the skis do not sink into the snow, but of great importance in softer snow. If the tips or tails are excessively weighted in soft snow, they will sink deeper into the snow and this will result in a braking action. Positions of extreme angulation or backweighting illustrated in the photographs in this book, almost universally on hard snow, are used to keep the skis carving *and* round out the end of a difficult turn, using the characteristics of the skis as much as possible to retain speed.

Proper forward-backward balance is very important in keeping the outside ski turning in carved turns just as it is in skidded turns. The search of many skiers for the ever elusive "neutral" position is inconsistent with the realities of changing forces, accelerations and compressions that occur during a turn across the fall line. In fact, there can be no such position as the skier must constantly move forward to balance acceleration and then backward to anticipate compression over the outside ski throughout the turn.

How is this done ? Ski teaching methods have traditionally recommended that the skier move the body forward or backward, usually from the ankle, although the knees and waist can give dramatic results as well. But the World Cup skiers do something radically different. They move the foot that they are weighting forward or backward underneath them throughout the turn. The timing and form can vary. Often the ankle is straight at the beginning of the turn, the knee pressed forward during the middle of the turn, and then the foot is pushed forward and the ankle straightened at the very end of the turn. This technique has the effect of moving the body forward or backward relative to the feet. Although this description seems rather complicated, the movement is easily recognized in the photomontages. The skiers take advantage of the greater mobility of the feet to correct and anticipate faster than if they had to move the entire body mass back and forth. Moving the feet under the body is a secret of World Cup skiing that can be exploited by all skiers to be quicker and achieve better balance.

By angulating for lateral stability and placing the feet for forward-backward effect, the skier can remain in balance over his edges. The ski will then turn by itself and the skier can steer the arc of the turn as desired. Virtually every World Cup giant slalom turn is driven in this way.

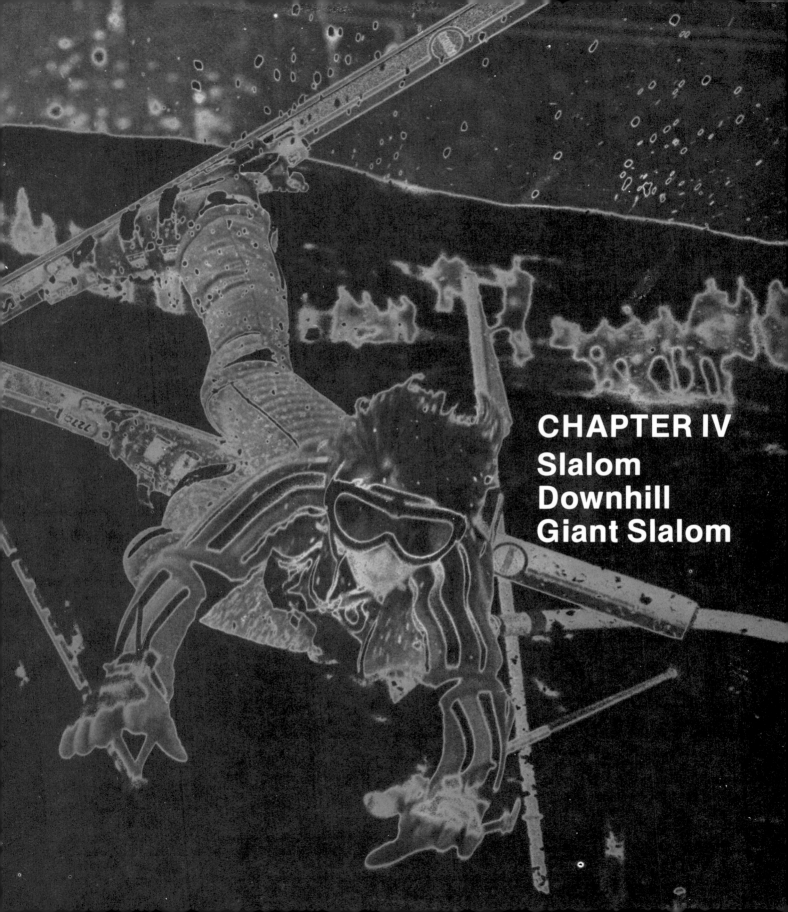

CHAPTER IV
**Slalom
Downhill
Giant Slalom**

Skiers who consciously train, working on their technique by free-skiing and especially by skiing gates and race courses and eventually racing at whatever level will become better sooner than skiers who do not. This is a fact of modern ski instruction. Besides discovering a new world of movement, a new motivation can be created and a sensation of living experienced that is difficult to obtain in daily life.

The turns of the world's best skiers are also the turns that *every* good skier should aspire to make, not just those interested in racing. For this reason, for our readers already racing, those who will start and everyone just interested, we have included and analysis of the disciplines of alpine skiing: slalom, downhill and giant slalom

SLALOM

A slalom race corresponds to free skiing approximately 60 short turns down an often steep and icy slope. It requires 50 to 60 seconds of intense involvement and concentration, much like a long sprint, but no really extreme fatigue as in the other disciplines. The skier must move more by reflex than by calculated or planned action. Nevertheless, great precision and control are necessary at all times and good sliding to minimize braking and allow the racer to carry as much speed as possible is essential to success.

Ingemar Stenmark, Sweden.
(following page) **Klaus Heidegger**, Austria.
1978 Madonna di Campiglio slalom.
Conditions: transition onto a very steep slope, fresh snow over ice.

Klaus Heidegger, Austria.
1978 Madonna di Campiglio slalom.
Conditions: transition onto a very steep slope, fresh snow over ice.

Two of the world's best slalom skiers are presented at 9 frames
per second in the same gates in the sequences on these and the
preceeding 2 pages. The skiers have just passed onto one of the
steepest sustained slopes of World Cup slalom. They demonstrate
near perfect balance over the outside ski through this difficult
transition. Stenmark's skis are carving so superbly that there is
exceptionally little spray coming from the edges of his outside ski
and none from the inside ski.

Heidegger's skis are also carving well, but not as exactly as
Stenmark's. In relation to fixed objects in the background, such as
trees and slalom poles, it is evident that in spite of the same speed
of entry into the transition by both skiers (during the first 5 pictures), Stenmark has gained approximately 30 centimeters over
Heidegger by the 8th photo of the sequence.

Ingemar Stenmark, Sweden *(upper photos)*.
Klaus Heidegger, Austria *(lower photos)*.
1978 Madonna di Campiglio slalom.

Stenmark's 30 cm. advantage over Heidegger gained in these two turns results from Heidegger's loosing contact with the snow by his outside ski in the 5th photo of the sequence. 11/100's of a second later, he is out of balance to the rear. This momentary fault decelerates Heidegger in relation to Stenmark. In this first World Cup slalom of 1978, Ingemar won, Heidegger was second.

Bojan Krizaj, Yugoslavia.
1978 Madonna di Campiglio slalom.

Through the same gates where we analyzed Ingemar Stenmark and Klaus Heidegger, we compare the third place skier Krizaj (above) with Phil Mahre on the following two pages. The photomontages clearly demonstrate the reason for the time differences between the skiers passing through these gates. They show Krizaj precisely after crossing the transition where he has suddenly lost pressure on his outside ski. His reaction to this is to maintain his low position and thrust both feet forward, particularly the outside foot, in order to maintain contact with the snow. Immediately after passing the transition, Phil Mahre vigorously sets his edges as evidenced by the snow spray from his skis. From this solid platform he extends and straightens his body.

Every section of a course requires an ultimate technical solution. In this particular case, the technique of Krizaj has enabled him to more effectively adapt to the demands of the situation.

Phil Mahre, USA.
1978 Madonna di Campiglio slalom.

Bojan Krizaj, Yugoslavia *(upper photos).*
Phil Mahre, USA *(lower photos).*

The skiers enter this series of gates with approximately the same speed, but by the last frame of the sequence Krizaj has gained a 40 cm. advantage over Mahre. This is unquestionably due to Mahre's deceleration from frame 4 to frame 5.

The slalom skier must often choose between edging or skidding techniques in order to maintain an equilibrium between his speed and control through the gate combinations.

Fausto Radici, Italy.
1978 Madonna di Campiglio slalom.

Radici, the winner of this race in 1977, is compared to the younger skier, Wenzel, who is shown on the following two pages. The skiers show remarkable similarity to the other champions in the preceeding photosequences from the waist up, and important differences from the waist down. Both Radici and Wenzel make exactly the same error over the transition, losing contact with the snow with their outside skis. Their relative speeds remain identical.

Andreas Wenzel, Lichtenstein.
1978 Madonna di Campiglio slalom.

Andreas Wenzel, Lichtenstein.
1978 Madonna di Campiglio slalom.

As both Radici and Wenzel have made the same error and have the same time through this sequence of gates, we concentrate on Wenzel to see what has taken place. Synchronized cameras view the same movements simultaneously, one facing the skier and the other from the side.

In the first two pictures, Wenzel has lost contact with the snow with his outside ski. Subsequently, he must edge very hard in order to regain control and his line. This is evidenced by his extremely angulated position in the lower right photo. When constant contact with the snow is maintained, this kind of excessive edging, which brakes the good sliding of the skis, can be avoided.

Ingemar Stenmark, Sweden.
1979 ARe slalom.
Conditions: soft snow and rutted course.

Skiing bumps

When skiing bumpy terrain, the ideal is to remain on the ground as much as possible. The ruts of a slalom course pose many of the same skiing problems as the moguls which every skier meets. The higher the skiers speed, the more the ruts or moguls tend to throw him into the air. To absorb and remain in control and in contact with the snow demands that the skier use the full range of motion in his joints. Notice that while the legs are moving up and down, the upper body remains comparatively stable.

Photo 1: The combination of his speed and a bump has projected Stenmark into the air. He has already fully extended his left leg in order for his outside ski to regain contact with the snow as soon as possible.

Photo 2: Stenmark executes a wide step as he exits the hole, assisted by a strong pole plant.

Photo 3: He has pulled his knees up to absorb the bump. This movement also anticipates the next hole, where he will have to extend to push his skis down.

Photo 4: Stenmark has extended his outside leg as he approaches the bottom of the hole.

Photos 5&6: Skiing out of the rut, Stenmark bends lower and lower to absorb the bank at the end of the hole. By pushing his outside foot forward, he can bend his knees even lower.

Klaus Heidegger, Austria (top series).
Paul Frommelt, Lichtenstein (middle series).
Toshiro Kaiwa, Japan (lower series).
1978 Kitzbuhel slalom.
Conditions: Hard, old snow and ice.

Heidegger, the winner of this race, is compared to two other top slalom skiers during the first run of the 1978 Kitzbuhel slalom. This particular section of the course caused most of the competitors of the first group to abandon the race. Consequently, compare the skiers' movements of the arms and skipoles, angulation-anticipation, unweighting and the use of turning forces. Of particular interest is their forward-backward balance through the series.

DOWNHILL

Downhill is the premier event of alpine ski racing. It is basic; namely the search for the fastest line down the mountain. Speeds up to 130 kilometers per hour are commonplace. The downhill embodies the thrill of sliding that instinctively delights every skier.

Downhill is similar to giant slalom in duration, but with much higher speed. Since downhill courses customarily have long straight traverses and schusses instead of continuous linked turns, as in giant slalom, the downhiller can better calculate his movements to achieve correct timing and line.

Characteristic to downhill skiing is the aerodynamic crouch or "egg" position. This is a very static position of the body and the constant muscle contraction necessary to maintain it inhibits the free flow of oxygen carrying blood to the muscle fibers, thereby exaggerating the fatigue normally associated with skiing.

Downhill racing equipment is also very specialized: 223 cm. and 215 cm. long skis for the men and women respectively, and softer, lower competition boots are standard.

Franz Klammer, Austria.
1978 Kitzbuhel downhill.

Walter Vesti, Switzerland.
1978 Kitzbuhel downhill.

The downhill at Kitzbuhel demands more of an alpine skier than
any other race of the World Cup circuit. When the conditions are icy,
as they were here, the "Steilhang" presents extreme technical difficulties. The Steilhang is a steep, narrow, bumpy and usually icy fall-
away turn where the sun never shines. It is a favorite place for spectators and often the subject of the skiers' night mares. The absolute
elite, however, represented by Walter Vesti, who posted the fastest
intermediate time, and frequent winner Franz Klammer, are able to
master the difficulties through ultimate technique.

Although the ideal in ski technique is a round, carved turn, this is
impossible over the Steilhang. As the skiers enter the pitch, they
inevitably bounce down the ice, even though they are well balanced
over their outside ski in a stable, wide stance. The arms move continually experiencing. Notice that as well as sliding forward, the
skiers are bouncing sideways, a result of the tremendous centrifugal
force.

Franz Klammer, Austria. *(upper series)*
Walter Vesti, Switzerland. *(lower series)*
1978 Kitzbuhel downhill. The "Steilhang".

To withstand the forces and remain in control of their speed and line, the skiers are obliged to maintain a position in the center of their skis. In spite of this, Vesti and Klammer must flex and extend their entire bodies to absorb the bumps and attempt to remain in contact with the snow. Even though Klammer and Vesti skied this section better than any of the other skiers, they are in the air as much as on the snow. The skis are no longer carving on the ice, but are ricochetting over it.

For the skier to have any directional control over his skis during the split second that they are in contact with the snow, he must be over his outside ski at all times.

The role of the arms in maintaining balance can not be emphasized enough. They are extended away from the body to provide greater leverage.

Gustavo Thoeni, Italy.
1978 Kitzbuhel downhill. The "Steilhang".

A top downhill racer needs extraordinary ability, both to win and to escape serious injury. By independent body movements, Thoeni achieves a sensational recovery on the infamous "steilhang", a recovery that was repeated in slow motion many times on European television.

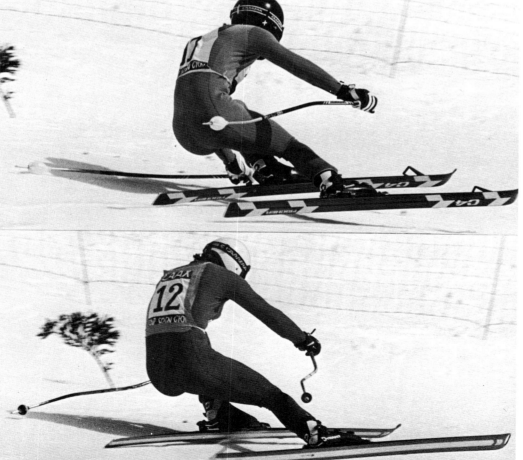

Steve Podborski, Canada (No. 17).
Josef Walcher, Austria (No. 12)
Erwin Josi, Switzerland (No. 15).

Werner Grissmann, Austria (No. 9).
Steve Podborski, Canada (No. 17).
Josef Walcher, Austria (No. 12).
Erwin Josi, Switzerland (No. 15).

The world's best downhill skiers all show striking similarities in their movements through the turns. Notice the hip angulation and the placement of their arms. The back is straight and the downhill leg is placed far out to the side.

In the first 5 photos of the sequence above, Grissmann appears to be moving his upper body progressively further back in relation to his skis. This is a result of the high speed turn and the fact that his skis have lost contact with the snow, but will allow him to immediately regain his balance upon landing and the reappearance of friction between the skis and the snow which will cause the skis to decelerate relative to his center of mass, which will subsequently move forward over his feet again.

1978 Arlberg-Kandahar downhill.

The downhill of the 1978 Arlberg-Kandahar was won by Ken Read with Dave Murray placing second. These photos were taken in Chamonix of the sweep by the two Canadian downhillers. Their approximate speed over these two sections was 120 kilometers per hour.

Ken Read, Canada. *(upper series)*
1978 Chamonix downhill.

Read prepares himself for the biggest jump of the course. To avoid being thrown by the lip of the jump he executes a classic pre-jump. With the speed he is carrying, Read is able to become airborn in 1/10 of a second by a vigorous bending of the waist, bringing the legs up and pushing the arms down and forward. Although the movement is relatively easy, the timing at high speed is extremely difficult, but Read demonstrates it here perfectly.

Dave Murray, Canada. *(lower series)*
1978 Chamonix downhill.

At high speed even a relatively slight roll in the terrain can give the skier a long flight through the air. With the incredible speed and size of this bump, it became one of the most spectacular obstacles of the course. Dave Murray's relaxed and superior balanced skiing make this passage look relatively easy. He enters the compression highly extended and then, 22/100's of a second later, he flexes as much as he can and still remain in balance. Murray continues his flight and progressive extension, which allow him to softly absorb the impact of the landing, always well balanced over his skis.

GIANT SLALOM

Giant slalom involves the control and precision of slalom with the speed and dimension of downhill. At first glance, the sweeping turns of giant slalom seem to be the most similar to free skiing of the alpine disciplines. But of the three, giant slalom is the event which most taxes the skiers' physical, technical and athletic qualities. The carved turns and perfect line of a World Cup giant slalom skier, unfortunately, bear little resemblance to what most skiers do when free skiing.

Good giant slalom skiing can be reduced to the search for one perfectly carved turn linked to another, from the top of the mountain to the bottom. The tendency among World Cup skiers is to become better at either slalom or downhill, and the rarity of the great giant slalom skier attests to the difficulty of achieving perfection in this discipline.

Ingemar Stenmark, Sweden. 1978 World Cup Final. Arosa, Switzerland.

Of all the photographs we've taken during the past two years, no other giant slalom turn was better executed that this one by Ingemar Stenmark. Although he starts the turn on very flat terrain that abruptly becomes steep and bumpy, he manages to maintain a perfect line and perfect contact with the snow with his outside ski. No snow can be seen flying off the inside ski at any point of the turn and only as he prepares to initiate the next turn does he step onto the right ski at the end of the sequence.

It is interesting to note how Stenmark keeps his hip into the hill (hip angulation) throughout the turn, yet there is mobility of the knee increasing and decreasing the edging of the ski and hence the form of the line. As Stenmark searches for the ideal line, his knee function resembles the steering wheel of a car as it laterally corrects the turn.

Gustavo Thoeni, Italy.
1977 Are giant slalom.

Thoeni begins the turn in a very relaxed, balanced and upright position and then pushes his feet forward into the turn. As the edging becomes more severe, he lowers smoothly, increasing his angulation. When letting the skis run, the feet are pushed in front of the skier, thereby weighting the heels, but when energetic edging becomes necessary, the body must come progressively forward over the center of the skis again.

Thoeni's forward push of the feet at the beginning of the turn is a reflex that anticipates the deceleration of the skis a moment later. The braking of the sliding of the skis is a result of the increased edging that follows. The momentum of the upper body carries it forward as the feet and skis slow down.

Immediately after passing the gate, Thoeni looks and calculates the line to the next gate and begins a powerful up-motion with his left leg.

Gustavo Thoeni, Italy.
1977 Are giant slalom.

Thoeni's dynamic lateral step enables him to radically change his inward lean from one turn to the next when it is combined, as it is here, with a complete weight change from one ski to the other. This is often the secret to effectively linked turns.

In the last three pictures of the sequence, Thoeni first establishes his inclination (or "bicycle lean") for the turn and then gradually increases his angulation. With such relaxed gestures, it is possible to ski the exact line necessary in giant slalom and retain maximum sliding of the skis, and thereby greater speed.

Andreas Wenzel, Lichtenstein.
1978 Waterville Valley giant slalom.

The photosequence of the 1978 Waterville Valley World Cup race winner Adreas Wenzel on this and the facing page is compared to the second place finisher, Ingemar Stenmark, on the following two pages. The important technical similarities that exist between all of the best skiers are evident as are the differences.

In the first two pictures to the left, both skiers are in very similar attitudes of strong angulation. The gate is set on top of a bump and as the skier's pass over this obstacle, Stenmark must release his knee angulation whereas Wenzel is able to maintain his and hold the best line. Regaining his knee angulation, Stenmark is able to round out the end of the turn and finishes it in practically the same place as Wenzel. Both skiers press hard on their outside skis throughout the turn, but especially just before stepping over to their left ski.

Ernst Good, Switzerland.
1977 Åre giant slalom.

Olympic gold and silver giant slalom medalists are compared during a World Cup race in Sweden. Throughout this sequence they show the remarkable technical similarity betwen giant slalom skiers of different ski teams that makes good skiing so international.

If a skier makes a lateral step that is too wide, he will encounter problems in dynamically shifting his weight from one ski to the other. In the 3rd and 4th figures in the sequence of Good above and of Thoeni on the facing page, the extended downhill leg of both skiers and their wide stances don't allow enough lateral momentum to transfer weighting to their right skis. But both skiers use the upward push of the bump to step from one ski to the other. Such an exaggerated step is rare, but demonstrates the complete adaptation of technique to terrain.

Gustavo Thoeni, Italy.
1977 Åre giant slalom.

As Thoeni completes the same turn described on the facing page, he looks ahead to anticipate what is coming.

Christa Kinshofer, West Germany.
1979 Aspen giant slalom.
Conditions: transition to flat terrain. Hard-packed snow.

Christa Kinshofer, at age 18, entered skiing's elite with five giant slalom victories and the 1979 giant slalom World Cup title. The key to her sudden rise in international racing is her advanced technique. The coordination of her movements gives her nearly perfect balance, which in turn allows her to ski elegantly and seemingly without effort.

Kinshofer free skis with her feet close together, a fact that has not escaped the attention of many ski technicians. With the aid of the camera it is possible to see that her skis are momentarily close together when not turning. It is also evident, however, that as soon as she begins to turn, her feet move further apart, as occurs with all top skiers.

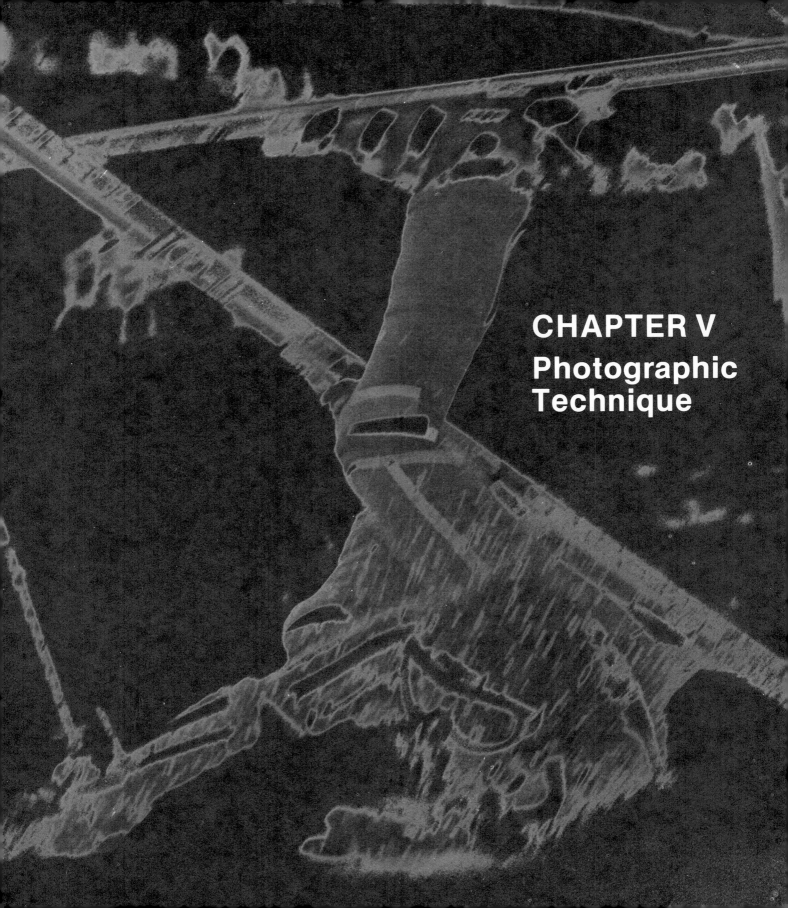

CHAPTER V
Photographic Technique

Before 1976 we had never taken a picture of a skier nor seen the inside of a darkroom. But it was evident to us that we could benefit in our profession as ski coaches from the possibilities of analyzing sports movements with 35mm. format motorized photography. As we progressed in our photographic ability, it became apaprent that we had something to offer all skiers. Over the next two seasons we took many thousands of pictures. In spite of the handicap of not being expert photographers, the fact that we are, by profession, alpine ski coaches made this book a possibility. With the eye of a trainer, we were able to choose camera angles which made the photographs very revealing.

Hours before the start of a World Cup race, we would be out with the racers, doing our own reconnaissance of the course. Owing to our training and experience as ski coaches, we could identify the interesting, difficult and decisive sections of the race. According to the position of the gates, the snow conditions and the terrain, as well as the estimated speed with which the racers would approach the section where we were filming, the technical elements that would be observed could be predicted. This a professional photographer can not do beyond a primitive level.

The photos that make up this work were selected from over 22,000 color and black and white negatives. These pictures were taken all over the world at World Cup races during the 1977, 1978 and 1979 seasons. The 1977 FIS World Championships at Garmisch-Partenkirchen, West Germany were also included for study. This work was performed at the same time that we were working, first in the racing service of the world's largest ski factory and later as coaches of the Canadian and Norwegian ski teams.

The most difficult problem in editing this work was deciding what to leave out! We tried to include only the best skiing by the best skiers. For this reason, many of the photos in this book were selected from the same races; Are, Sweden, Madonna di Campiglio, Italy and Kitzbuhel, Austria, for example. At these races we found a unique combination of exceptional snow conditions and good weather which made it possible for the skiers to fully express themselves and their technique.

Outside of this book, our photographs are helping to broaden the technical understanding of many coaches. Some of the photomontages are already being used for trainer education by the Ski Federations of Switzerland, Norway and Canada. It is our sincere hope that with the assistance of this book, many of our readers, as well, will be able to see and distinguish the interesting from the superficial in the gestures of a skier.

The pictures were taken exclusively with Nikon cameras equipped with motors to automatically advance the film. We benefited enormously from an exceptional camera which is not available commercially. It was specially built for us by Nikon of Japan, and has the ability to take up to 9 pictures per second, a picture every 11/100's of a second. The other Nikon cameras which we used take 5 pictures per second, or 20/100's of a second seperating each image. In general, the faster camera was used for downhill, because of the high speed of the skiers, while the slower motor speeds were used for slalom events. These motor speeds seem to correspond well to the speed of movement of the skiers and enabled us to observe their technique. Faster motors exist, but then the photomontage becomes cluttered with overlapping images showing movements so slight as to be irrelevant. At speeds over 9 images per second, half the photos have to be deleted in order to arrive at a coherent result.

The only lenses we used were the 50mm. normal and wide angle, and the Nikkor 80-200mm. zoom. No other lens filter, other than the ultraviolet, was used. We used Kodak Plus-X and Tri-X black and white film and Kodak Professional 200 Ektachrome color film. In the darkroom, we used Ilford photographic paper exclusively.

In spite of the often severe weather conditions, normal when working in the mountains during winter, not once did we experience equipment failure with any of the three cameras. In reality, the only practical limit to taking pictures was how cold the fingers got. At some locations this was an important factor as the air temperature dropped to -20° C.

During the slalom at Kitzbuhel, Austria, the last World Cup race before the 1978 FIS World Championships, we were able to employ a new photographic system which has never before been exploited in studying ski technique. Two motorized cameras were synchronized around the same combinations of gates. One camera filmed the skiers from above and behind and the other was positioned a little below and infront of the skiers. This allowed the technique of the skiers to be studied from two angles, front and back, at the same time and in the same place.

The matter of camera position is very important. It is certain that different angles of view bring into relief different aspects of a skier's movements. Over the past two seasons, we made an effort to film the techniques of the world's best skiers from every possible angle. Some were extremely difficult to achieve, such as the pictures taken from slightly above which show the skiers' angulation so well and the pivoting of their skis. Certainly some camera positions give more dramatic results than others, but the photographs included in this study were selected not for their dramatic impact but because they best portray the movements and techniques of the virtuoso skiers of the world alpine elite.

EPILOG

Alpine skiing, the sport we all enjoy so much and which has and shall give so many satisfactory moments, is being practiced by more and more people. What values are of importance to these enthusiasts? The learning factor, the progression of one's own ability as a skier, is of great interest to most. Certainly the development of solid technical skills has its place. There can be nasty moments at the very beginning stages of learning to ski; getting wet from falling in the snow, fright, etc. This gives the beginner one primary concern: improving fast because of all the inconvenience he has to experience. But this is not an everlasting period and what should come first is having fun.

The ability to enjoy skiing doesn't always depend on the skier's technical competence. It's not uncommon to hear skiers say, "I really like to ski, but I'm not very good", as if this is an excuse for being a poor skier. Simply being a more skilled skier doesn't mean having greater pleasure. In fact, the contrary is often true. The average skier who can only ski on weekends, or less, is often more enthusiastic about skiing and derives more enjoyment from it than the world's elite racers. And since alpine skiing is a game for children, let's let it be as it is with children: having fun.